GW00496776

CHILTI WALKS

BUCKINGHAMSHIRE

Nick Moon

This book is one of a series of three which provide a comprehensive coverage of walks throughout the whole of the Chiltern area (as defined by the Chiltern Society). The walks included vary in length from 2.3 to 10.8 miles, but are mainly in the 5- to 7-mile range popular for half-day walks, although suggestions of possible combinations of walks are given for those preferring a full day's walk.

Each walk text gives details of nearby places of interest and is accompanied by a specially drawn map of the route which also indicates local pubs and a skeleton road network.

The author, Nick Moon, has lived in or regularly visited the Chilterns all his life and has, for 25 years, been an active member of the Chiltern Society's Rights of Way Group, which seeks to protect and improve the area's footpath and bridleway network. Thanks to the help and encouragement of the late Don Gresswell MBE, he was introduced to the writing of books of walks and has since written or contributed to a number of publications in this field.

The Chiltern Society

OTHER PUBLICATIONS BY NICK MOON

Chiltern Walks Trilogy
Chiltern Walks 1: Hertfordshire, Bedfordshire and North
                          Buckinghamshire: Book Castle (new edition) 1996
Chiltern Walks 2: Buckinghamshire: Book Castle: (new editon) 1997
Chiltern Walks 3: Oxfordshire and West Buckinghamshire:
                          Book Castle (new edition) 1996

Family Walks
Family Walks 1: Chilterns – South: Book Castle 1997
Family Walks 2: Chilterns – North: due 1998

Oxfordshire Walks
Oxfordshire Walks 1: Oxford, The Cotswolds and The Cherwell Valley:
                              Book Castle 1994
Oxfordshire Walks 2: Oxford, The Downs and The Thames Valley:
                              Book Castle 1995

Complete Books
Walks for Motorists: Chilterns (Southern Area): Frederick Warne 1979
Walks for Motorists: Chilterns (Northern Area): Frederick Warne 1979
Walks in the Hertfordshire Chilterns: Shire 1986

Contributions
Chiltern Society Footpath Maps: a number of walk descriptions –
                                    also all map checking since c.1975
Walks in the Countryside round London: W. Foulsham & Co Ltd. 1985
Walker's Britain: Pan 1982
Walker's Britain II: Pan 1986

First published May 1991
New edition July 1997
by The Book Castle
12 Church Street, Dunstable, Bedfordshire

© Nick Moon

Computer Typeset by 'Keyword', Aldbury, Herts
Printed in Great Britain by Antony Rowe Ltd., Chippenham

ISBN 1 871199 43 3

Contents

POSSIBLE LONGER WALKS PRODUCED BY COMBINING WALKS DESCRIBED IN THE BOOK

Walks	Miles	Km
1 + 16	12.7	20.5
1 + 16 + 17	18.8 or 18.4	30.2 or 29.6
4 + 5	11.9	19.2
4 + 5 + 6	20.5	33.1
5 + 6	15.9	25.7
9 + 11	18.6	30.0
10 + 11	16.4 or 16.6	26.4 or 26.8
13 + 15	11.1	17.8
13 + 19	9.9	15.9
13 + 19 + 15	15.3	24.7
16 + 17	12.2	19.7
20 + 28A	16.5	26.6
20 + 28B	14.2	22.9
21 + 25	12.0	19.4
25 + 26	18.3	29.5
26 + 29	16.1	25.9
26 + 29 + 27	22.7 or 22.0	36.5 or 35.4
27 + 29	14.0 or 13.3	22.5 or 21.4

Introduction

This book of walks is one of three covering the whole of the Chilterns from the Goring Gap on the River Thames to the Hitchin Gap in North Hertfordshire. As the Buckinghamshire Chilterns account for well over a third of the Chiltern area, it has proved necessary to omit certain parts of them from this volume, as only in this way could a reasonably equitable spread of the walks across the Chilterns be achieved. The area to the west of a line from Princes Risborough to Marlow is included in the volume covering the Oxfordshire and West Buckinghamshire Chilterns, while the detached area around Ivinghoe is to form part of the Hertfordshire, Bedfordshire and North Buckinghamshire volume. Nevertheless the area which remains, extending from the escarpment between Princes Risborough and Tring in the northwest to the Thames and Colne valleys in the south and east, is one of considerable variety, with a whole series of inviting landscapes to be explored.

On the northwestern edge, there is the escarpment, parts of which are very steep, where woodland is interspersed with spectacular downland. Progressing southeastwards, to the east of the Wendover Gap, there is probably the remotest part of the Buckinghamshire Chilterns in the form of the typical Chiltern ridge and bottom country around The Lee and Cholesbury, while to the south of this Gap is the Hampden Country, where one again finds the characteristic Chiltern ridges and bottoms but in a more wooded setting. To the east of Chesham is an upland plateau more typical of Hertfordshire, but bounded by deep valleys which add variety to its walks, while, to the south of Amersham, the wooded hills of the Penn country offer a surprising sense of remoteness when one considers that they are a mere 25 miles from Central London. On the eastern boundary, the ridge separating the Misbourne and Colne valleys also offers some quiet rural areas with extensive views to the east and south and even the Colne valley with its flooded gravel pits and the Grand Union Canal has much to offer for those interested in boats or water fowl. To the south of the A40 and M40, the wide section of the Thames valley between Marlow and Cookham also has much to offer the walker with its picturesque riverside, extensive views from the surrounding hills and attractive areas of woodland on its slopes, while the heavily-wooded plateau to the east around Burnham Beeches and Stoke Poges, interspersed with pleasant shallow bottoms, thanks to the visual and sound-proofing protection of its beautiful woods, also provides plenty of scope for agreeable walks despite its proximity to Slough and the metropolis.

The majority of walks included in this book are in the 5 – 7 mile range, which is justifiably popular for half-day walks, but, for the less energetic or for short winter afternoons, a few shorter versions are indicated in the text, while others can be devised with the assistance of a map. In addition, a number of walks in the 7 – 10 mile range are included for those preferring a leisurely day's walk or for longer spring and summer afternoons, while a list of possible combinations of walks is provided for those favouring a full day's walk of between 10 and 23 miles.

Details of how to reach the starting points by car and where to park are given in the introductory information to each walk and any convenient railway stations are shown on the accompanying plan. For information on bus services telephone 0345–382000.

All the walks described here follow public rights of way, use permissive paths across land owned by public bodies or cross public open space. As the majority of walks cross land used for economic purposes such as agriculture, forestry or the rearing of game, walkers are urged to follow the Country Code at all times:

- Guard against all risk of fire
- Fasten all gates
- Keep dogs under proper control
- Keep to the paths across farmland
- Avoid damaging fences, hedges and walls
- Leave no litter – take it home
- Safeguard water supplies
- Protect wild life, wild plants and trees
- Go carefully on country roads on the right-hand side facing oncoming traffic
- Respect the life of the countryside

Observing these rules helps prevent financial loss to landowners and damage to the environment, as well as the all-too-frequent and sometimes justified bad feeling towards walkers in the countryside.

While it is hoped that the special maps provided with each walk will assist the user to complete the walks without going astray and skeleton details of the surrounding road network are given to enable walkers to shorten the routes in emergency, it is always advisable to take an Ordnance Survey or Chiltern Society map with you to enable you to shorten or otherwise vary the routes without using roads or get your bearings if you do become seriously lost. Details of the appropriate maps are given in the introductory information of each walk.

As for other equipment, readers are advised that where mud warnings are given, the walks are those on which mud remains in dry weather. At other times, all walks are subject to some mud. In any event, proper walking boots are to be recommended at all times, as, even when there are no mud problems, hard ruts or rough surfaces make the protection given by boots to the ankles desirable. In addition, the nature of the countryside makes any Chiltern paths prone to overgrowth, particularly in summer. To avoid resultant discomfort to walkers, protective clothing is advisable, especially where specific warnings are given.

Some of the walks may be familiar to readers as they were previously published in the 'Walks for Motorists' Chilterns volumes which are now out of print, but about half are completely new or have been radically altered, while all of the old walks have been rechecked and brought up to date. In addition, as the walks are now appearing in the Chiltern Society's name, all the path numbers have been shown on the plans and incorporated into the texts. These numbers, which are also shown on the Society's Footpath Maps, consist of the official County Council footpath number with the prefix letters used by the Society to indicate the parish concerned. It is therefore most helpful to use these when reporting any path problems you may find, together, if possible, with the national grid reference for the precise location of the trouble spot, as, in this way, the problem can be identified on the ground with a minimum of loss of time in looking for it. National grid references can, however, only be calculated with the help of Ordnance Survey Landranger, Explorer or Pathfinder maps and an explanation of how this is done can be found in the Key to all Landranger or Explorer maps.

The length of time required for any particular walk depends on a number of factors such as your personal walking speed, the number of hills, stiles etc. to be negotiated, whether or not you stop to rest, eat or drink, investigate places of interest etc. and the number of impediments such as mud, crops, overgrowth, ploughing etc. which you encounter, but generally an average speed of between two and two and a half miles per hour is about right in the Chilterns. It is, however, always advisable to allow extra time if you are limited by the daylight or catching a particular bus or train home in order to avoid your walk developing into a race against the clock.

Should you have problems with any of the paths used on the walks or find that the description given is no longer correct, the author would be most grateful if you could let him have details (c/o The Book Castle), so that attempts can be made to rectify the problem or the text can be corrected at the next reprint. Nevertheless, the author hopes that you will not encounter any serious problems and have pleasure from following the walks.

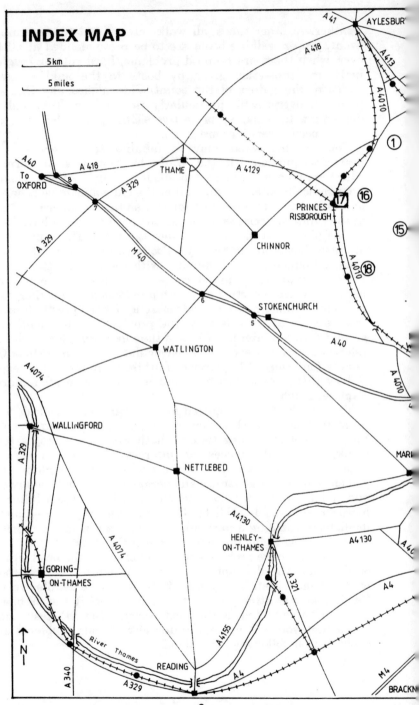

INDEX MAP

5 km

5 miles

AYLESBUR'
A 41
A 418
A413
A4010
①
A40 To OXFORD
A 418
A 329
THAME
A 4129
PRINCES RISBOROUGH
⑯
⑰
⑮
8
7
A 329
M40
CHINNOR
A4010
⑱
6
5
STOKENCHURCH
A40
A4010
WATLINGTON
A4074
A 329
WALLINGFORD
NETTLEBED
MARI
A4130
A4130
A4
HENLEY-ON-THAMES
A4074
A 321
GORING-ON-THAMES
A4155
M4
River Thames
A 340
READING
A329
A4
BRACKN
N

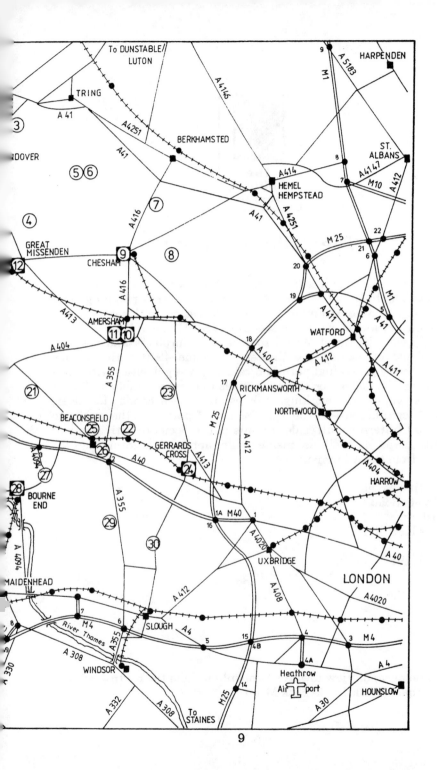

The Chiltern Society

The Chiltern Society

The Chiltern Society was founded in 1965 with the objects: 'To encourage high standards of town and country planning and architecture and to stimulate public interest in and care for the beauty, history and character of the area of the Chiltern Hills.'

The Society Rights of Way Group actively protects and restores public rights of way in the Chilterns – some 4900 paths. It has surveyed every individual path and takes up irregularities with local parish councils, district or county councils to preserve public rights. It organises voluntary working parties most weekends to clear, waymark or otherwise encourage the use of paths for the public to enjoy the Chiltern countryside. Details of the Society's activities and footpath maps as well as membership application forms can be obtained from the Administrator:

Christine Knight,
113 Vale Road
Chesham
Bucks HP5 3HP

(Tel: 01494–771250)

Cover Photograph: View towards Bradenham from the northwest at harvest time, (Walk 18). © Nick Moon

WALK 1: Ellesborough (Butler's Cross)

Length of Walk: 6.2 miles / 10.0 Km

Starting Point: Crossroads by 'Russell Arms' and
Ellesborough Village Hall at Butler's Cross.

Grid Ref: SP843070

Maps: OS Landranger Sheet 165
OS Explorer Sheet 2
(or old Pathfinder Sheet 1118 (SP80/90))
Chiltern Society FP Map No. 3

How to get there/Parking: Butler's Cross, 1.7 miles west
of Wendover, may be reached from the town by following
the Princes Risborough road for 1.7 miles to a crossroads
by the 'Russell Arms' at Butler's Cross. Here turn right
into Chalkshire Road and look for a suitable place to park.

Ellesborough, at the foot of the Chiltern escarpment, consists
of a series of hamlets connected by ribbons of development,
one of which is Butler's Cross where the village pub, shop and
post office and the village hall are situated. Despite its small
population, the parish is of national significance as it contains
Chequers, the country retreat of prime ministers and the
imposing fifteenth-century parish church on its prominent
hillock at the foot of Beacon Hill is regularly attended by
prime ministers and has also played host to various foreign
statesmen.

The walk explores this parish which can boast some of the
most spectacular scenery in the Chilterns, soon climbing to
the summit of Coombe Hill with its panoramic views of the
surrounding hills and the Vale of Aylesbury before continuing
through characteristic Chiltern woodland to the ridgetop
village of Dunsmore. It then proceeds through more woodland
to enter Chequers Park at Buckmoorend. Having passed the
house at a distance, you circle the slopes of Beacon Hill with
more fine views, before returning via Ellesborough church to
Butler's Cross.

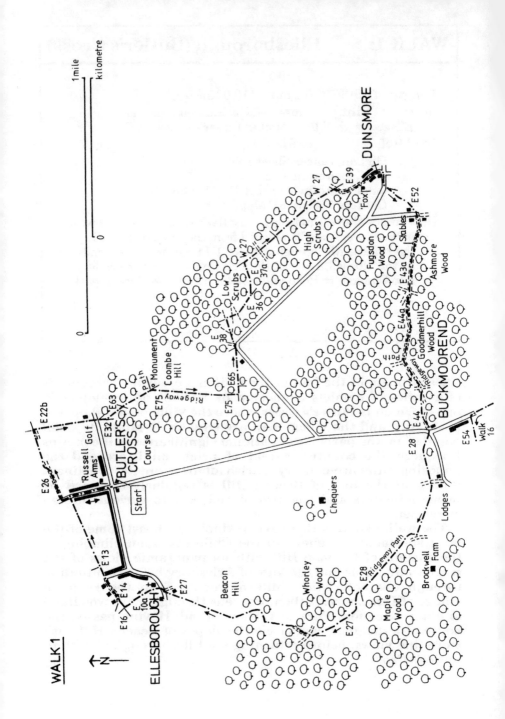

WALK 1

1mile
kilometre

0

0

N

ELLESBOROUGH

E16
E14
E 10a
E27

E13

'Russell
Arms'
Golf
Course

'Russell
Arms'

E26

E22b

BUTLER'S
CROSS

Start

E32
E63

Coombe
Hill Monument

E75

path

path

Ridgeway

Ridgeway

E75
E65

E
38

E
36 37a

W 27

Low
Scrubs

High
Scrubs

W 27

W 27

'Fox'

E39

DUNSMORE

E52

Stables

Fugsdon
Wood

E 43a

Ashmore
Wood

E44a

Goodmerhill
Wood

Ridgeway Path

E 44

E 28

BUCKMOOREND

E54

Walk
16

Lodges

Chequers

Beacon
Hill

Whorley
Wood

E28

Ridgeway Path

Maple
Wood

E27

Brockwell
Farm

12

Starting from the crossroads by the 'Russell Arms' and Ellesborough Village Hall, take Chalkshire Road. After some 350 yards, shortly before a right-hand bend, turn right over a stile by a gate and follow a farm track (path E26) across a field, then between a hedge and a fence to a gate. Here fork left leaving the track and following a right-hand fence straight on to a stile at the far end of the field. Cross this and turn right onto path E22b following a right-hand fence uphill to a stile onto Ellesborough Golf Course. Having crossed this, follow a right-hand hedge straight on. Where the hedge turns right, leave it and continue straight on through a group of trees and between two areas of dense scrub. Now pass just right of the clubhouse to a hedge gap onto the Wendover road.

Cross this busy road carefully and take the right-hand of two bridleways (E32) straight on through gates on the edge of woodland, then immediately fork left onto path E63, climbing through a squeeze-stile into the woodland. The path becomes progressively steeper and on leaving the woodland, becomes steeper still before reaching the monument at the summit of Coombe Hill erected in 1901 in memory of soldiers killed in the Boer War.

After stopping to admire the superb panoramic views from this point 852 feet above sea level, pass right of the monument and take the Ridgeway Path (E75) keeping right of the bushes ahead and continuing just below the ridgetop for over a third of a mile until you reach a fenceline. Here turn left onto path E65 following the fenceline uphill and ignoring a stile in it where the Ridgeway Path turns off. Where the ground levels out, continue to follow the fenceline, which is concealed by bushes in places, until you reach gates into a car park at a bend in the Dunsmore road.

Here go through a small gate and bear half left across the car park to a squeeze-stile leading into coppiced beech woodland known as Low Scrubs. Now follow a winding waymarked path (E38), keeping left at a fork and soon reaching a waymarked crossing path. Turn right onto this path (E36) and follow it for nearly 300 yards ignoring all crossing and branching paths. On reaching a second large brackeny clearing, turn left at a waymarked junction onto path E37a into woodland and follow this well-defined path until you reach an old iron fence. Here turn right and follow path W27 alongside this fence for half a mile, disregarding various junctions and later with fences on both sides. On crossing a stile where the first cottage at Dunsmore comes into view ahead, fork right onto a fenced track (bridleway E39) and follow it into Dunsmore.

On reaching the end of a village street by the 'Fox', follow it straight on for some 200 yards to a crossroads. Here turn right onto the major road. After about 90 yards turn left over a stile by a gate onto path

E52. Bear half right downhill to a stile in the bottom corner of the field. Having crossed this, continue straight on downhill, crossing four further stiles, to reach the end of a road by stables in the valley bottom. Cross the end of this road and take a stony track (bridleway E43a) straight on, soon entering Ashmore Wood. After one third of a mile, at a four-way fork, take path E44a straight on up the valley bottom, soon climbing to cross a ridge. Here the path turns somewhat to the left and you disregard a branching path to the right and continue downhill (now on the Ridgeway Path again) to a waymarked crossways near the edge of the wood. Take bridleway E44 straight on into a finger of woodland, soon forking right through a squeeze-stile onto a segregated footpath. After rejoining the bridleway, keep straight on to reach a road junction at Buckmoorend.

Cross the major road and go through a kissing-gate opposite onto path E28 into Chequers Park, then bear slightly left across the park to a telegraph pole. Here bear half left to kissing-gates flanking the main drive. Go through these and a further kissing-gate then bear half right to a stile at a corner of Maple Wood. Cross this and turn right following a fenced path along the outside edge of the wood to an old gate, where there is a good, but distant view of Chequers itself.

Built on the site of an older house by Sir William Hawtrey in 1565, Chequers Court (as it used to be known) was presented to the nation by Lord Lee of Fareham in 1917 for the purpose of providing a country retreat for prime ministers and has served that purpose ever since.

Now continue to follow the outside edge of Maple Wood to reach a kissing-gate near a corner of the park. Go through this and fork right through some bushes to join the outside edge of Whorley Wood, then follow it for a quarter of a mile (now on E27) until you reach a gate and stile into the wood. Cross the stile and a macadam drive and take a woodland track straight on, gradually bearing right. On leaving the wood, bear half left across a field to a signposted path through scrub, descending a series of rough steps and then following the contours of Beacon Hill to a stile. Now follow an obvious path across open downland rounding the hill to reach a stile, then head for Ellesborough Church to reach a kissing-gate onto the Wendover road opposite a row of thatched cottages.

Turn right along the road, then, at a bus stop, cross the road and take a macadam path (E10a) up a slope to a gate into the churchyard. Inside the churchyard, leave the macadam path and follow the left-hand wall past the church tower, soon descending a series of steps. Where the steps turn left, leave them and continue straight on through a kissing-gate and descend steeply to a stile. Cross this and continue straight on across a field to a gate and stile. Do not cross this stile, but instead turn right onto path E16 and follow a left-hand fence crossing two stiles to reach the end of Springs Lane by a cottage. Take this lane (path E14) straight on past several cottages and a farm. Where the lane turns right, leave it bearing slightly right and taking a green lane right of a hydrant (path E13) straight on into a field. Here follow what is usually a crop break to a stile, then continue between fences to a stile onto Chalkshire Road. Turn right along this road and retrace your steps to your starting point.

WALK 2: Wendover

Length of Walk: 5.3 miles / 8.5 Km

Starting Point: Clocktower at northeastern end of Wendover High Street

Grid Ref: SP870099

Maps: OS Landranger Sheet 165
OS Explorer Sheet 2 (or old Pathfinder Sheets 1094 (SP81/91) & 1118 (SP80/90))
Chiltern Society FP Map No. 18

Parking: Adequate on- or off-street parking in or near town centre

Notes: The descent from Haddington Hill tends to be slippery.

Wendover, an ancient borough on the Upper Icknield Way at one of the few real gaps in the Chiltern Escarpment, would seem to be a settlement of considerable antiquity. Not only is it located on an ancient road, but also Iron Age pottery was found there and its name is of Celtic origin deriving from 'Gwyn-dwfr' meaning 'holy' or 'fair water'. Today the centre of the town retains its old world charm thanks to a wealth of Georgian shops and houses as well as a number of older cottages and some fine trees.

The walk caters for all tastes, leaving Wendover by way of the towpath of the disused Wendover Arm of the Grand Union Canal and following this to Halton. It then crosses Halton Park and returns via the wooded heights of Haddington Hill, where there are fine views of the Vale of Aylesbury.

Starting from the clocktower at the northeastern end of Wendover High Street, take Aylesbury Road for some 300 yards, then turn right into Wharf Road. Follow this for about 200 yards to a gap in the houses on the left by No.41. Just past this house, turn left through a gap onto W12, the towpath of the Wendover Arm Canal at the end of this canal built in the 1790s. Now follow the towpath (later H19, WT36 & H19 again) along the left bank of the disused canal for 1.7 miles leaving the town behind. After one mile, pass under a road bridge, then, on reaching a second bridge, the path leads you onto the road at Halton village.

Turn right onto this road, crossing the canal bridge, and follow it to a right-hand bend just past a bus shelter. Here turn left through the gates

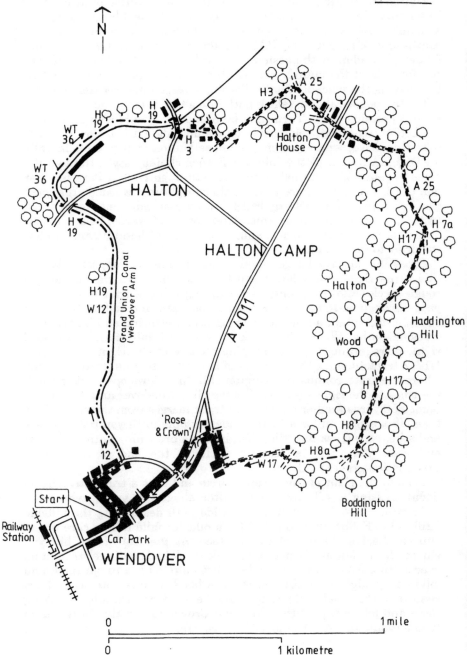

of Halton churchyard onto H3 leading to Halton church, built in 1813. The immaculately maintained churchyard contains a large number of airmen's graves bearing witness to Halton's long-standing and continuing links with the RAF. By the church, bear half right and follow a macadam path passing right of the church to a kissing-gate at the far side of the churchyard. Go through this gate, then bear half left leaving the macadam path. Passing a large lime tree and keeping left of the houses ahead, take a path into a belt of trees and follow it to a stony crossing track. Turn right onto this track and follow it through the belt of trees until you emerge onto a macadam drive. Now turn left onto this drive, where you may glimpse Halton House, built in 1884 for Baron Alfred de Rothschild in a French chateau style, through the trees to your right and follow the drive through Halton Park for over one third of a mile. Where it turns sharp right in a wooded area, pass through a gap in a post-and-rail fence onto an adjacent rough track (A25) and turn right along this. After some 250 yards, bear half left onto another macadam drive, and, ignoring a left-hand turning, follow the drive to the A4011.

Cross this fast road carefully and take a side-road opposite. Where this turns right into a housing estate, continue straight on along a rough track (A25) to a gate. Disregarding a horse trail to the right, pass through a squeeze-stile beside the gate and follow the track straight on for half a mile bearing right at a clearing and ignoring all crossing paths. Where the track (now H7a) finally forks, bear half right, disregarding a path dropping steeply to the right, and follow H17, a track hugging the contours of the hill. After one third of a mile, where the track rounds Haddington Hill, fine views open out through the trees to the right towards Coombe Hill, Wendover and Aylesbury. Some 350 yards further on, another track merges from the right. Here take H8 straight on for a further quarter mile until you reach a gate and stile. Now cross the stile, then ignore a branching path to the left and soon you reach a turning circle at the end of a Forestry Commission gravel road.

Pass to the right of the turning circle and take a track straight on (H8a) crossing a stile by a gate. After about 100 yards, where the track forks, bear half right onto a wide path descending the hillside (still H8a). Follow this downhill for a quarter mile taking care not to slip on the treacherous chalky surface. At the foot of the hill you emerge from Halton Wood, cross a wide track and continue straight on over a stile. After a few yards, bear left onto W17, a rough road, and follow it straight on until you reach a bend in an estate road. Turn right onto this road and follow it to its end. Here turn left into Tring Road and follow it past the 'Rose and Crown' to join the A4011, then turn left onto this for Wendover town centre.

WALK 3:   Aston Hill

Length of Walk: 5.7 miles / 9.2 Km (excluding detour to cairn)

Starting Point: Aston Hill car park.

Grid Ref: SP891101

Maps: OS Landranger Sheet 165
           OS Explorer Sheet 2 (or old Pathfinder Sheets
           1094 (SP81/91) & 1118 (SP80/90))
           Chiltern Society FP Map No. 18

How to get there/Parking: From Tring town or bypass
take the A41 westwards, then after half a mile turn left
onto the A4011 towards Wendover. After a further
three-quarters of a mile turn left again onto a road to
Cholesbury and follow it for half a mile to Aston Hill
picnic site and car park at the top of the hill.

Aston Hill, part of the escarpment above Aston Clinton from
which it derives its name, marks the northern end of the
heavily wooded ridge which includes the highest point in the
Chilterns. From this vantage point, there is a fine view over
Wilstone Reservoir and the Vale of Aylesbury towards
Mentmore Towers on its prominent ridge about six miles to
the north. This mansion, built for Baron Mayer de Rothschild
in 1852 by Sir Joseph Paxton, designer of the Crystal Palace,
was for nearly a century the home of the Earls of Rosebery
including a late nineteenth century prime minister and is now
the property of the Transcendental Meditation Cult. Wendover
Woods, as much of this woodland is collectively known, belong
to the Forestry Commission which has gone to considerable
lengths to provide recreational facilities in the area,
particularly for the walker.

The walk, as well as traversing a considerable amount of
woodland, descends the escarpment into farmland near Tring,
visits the Hertfordshire hilltop hamlet of Hastoe and,
optionally, the cairn marking the Chiltern summit.

Starting from Aston Hill car park, turn left onto the road, then after a
few yards, opposite a cottage, turn left onto footpath A13, a track into
the woods. Follow it for a third of a mile, ignoring branching tracks
and paths to the left and passing a field to the right, to reach the

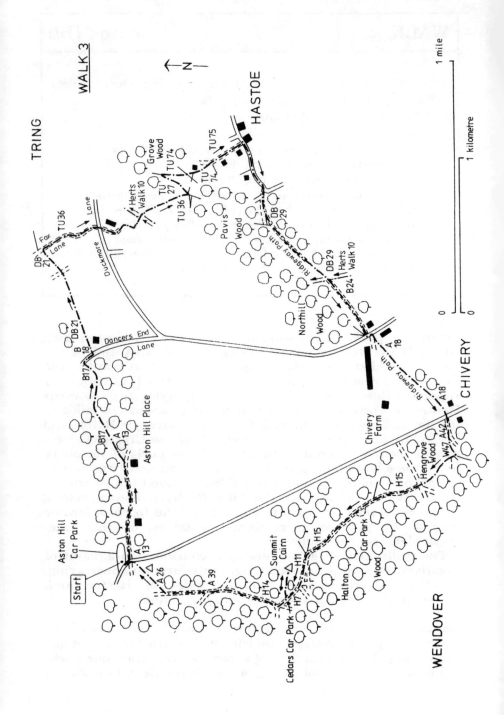

WALK 3

TRING

HASTOE

WENDOVER

CHIVERY

1 mile

1 kilometre

gated drive to Aston Hill Place. Here cross a stile to the left of the gate and follow a well-defined path (later B17) through the woods, gradually descending for half a mile (later with fine views towards Tring Reservoirs, Mentmore Towers and Ivinghoe Beacon), until you reach a road called Dancers End Lane. Turn right onto this, and just past a left-hand gate turn left onto B18, a narrow hedged path. After 100 yards the path emerges into a field. Here take path DB21 following the left-hand hedge and crossing a track and stile at the far end of the field. Now follow the left-hand hedge straight on to byway TU36, a green lane following the county boundary called Fox Lane. Turn right into this and follow it for quarter of a mile to reach a road called Duckmore Lane. Having crossed this, continue straight on along a rough lane (still TU36) to a cottage where it narrows to a path. Follow this straight on for a further third of a mile, ignoring a crossing path (the route of Herts. Walk 10) and later entering Grove Wood.

About 80 yards into the wood, by the corner of a right-hand field, turn sharp left onto TU27, a path which climbs at first, then levels out as a ledge following the contours of the hill. After a few yards, go straight on at a fork following a terraced path along the contours until you reach a T-junction. Here turn sharp right onto TU74, a wide path climbing the hill. At the top, leave the wood by a hedged path to emerge onto a rough road (TU75). Follow this straight on to a macadam road at the hamlet of Hastoe.

Turn right onto this road and follow it to a sharp left-hand bend. Here leave the road, bearing slightly right, ignoring a bridleway to the right and going through the smaller of two gates to enter Pavis Wood. Now follow the Ridgeway Path (DB29) straight on. After about 120 yards where the track forks, take the left-hand option and keep straight on along the inside edge of the wood with fine views out into the Vale of Aylesbury through the trees to your right ignoring branching paths to the right. At one point the track narrows to a path through a plantation, then, at a waymarked crossways (where you recross Herts. Walk 10), take B24, a wider muddy timber-track straight on along the inside edge of Northill Wood for quarter of a mile to reach a road. Turn left onto this road, leaving the woodland. After a few yards, opposite double gates, turn right over a stile at the left-hand corner of the entrance to a farm track, then take path A18, crossing a field diagonally to a stile right of a small copse in the hollow ahead. Cross this stile and follow the edge of the copse, later a left-hand hedge, to a stile leading onto a road by one of the scattered cottages at Chivery.

Cross this road and take a bridleway opposite (A42) into Hengrove Wood. Where this bridleway forks, take the right-hand option (W47), descending into a sunken gully, then where this turns to the left and starts to drop down, turn right up another gully. Ignoring a left-hand path and horse-trail, follow a permissive path beside a right-hand boundary ridge, passing through a squeeze-stile and continuing for some 300 yards to a bend in a Forestry Commission road. Follow this road (H15, later H11) straight on through Halton Wood for two-thirds of a mile to where the road forks. Here leave the main road and take a stony track straight on, soon stepping over a low wooden barrier and passing a tall cedar with two benches beneath it. Now bear slightly right onto path H7 along a grassy clearing, soon crossing another low wooden barrier to enter a car park. At this point you are on a level ridge top which at 876 feet above sea-level is the highest point in the Chilterns and if you take a path through the trees to your right, you will soon reach the cairn at the edge of the wood marking the Chiltern summit.

Otherwise go straight on, rejoining the road, then bearing right onto H14 and continue along it for a further third of a mile. Where the road turns left and starts to descend, take path A39 straight on at a fork, leaving the macadamed road, with a view through the trees to the left over Wendover towards Coombe Hill and out into the Vale of Aylesbury. About 50 yards before reaching a gate, turn right onto path A26 to a stile out of the wood. Cross this and bear half left across a field, keeping left of a concrete triangulation post to a stile leading in a few yards to a road, where Aston Hill car park is a few yards to the left.

WALK 4:   The Lee

Length of Walk: 5.5 miles / 8.8 Km
Starting Point: 'Cock & Rabbit', The Lee village green.
Grid Ref: SP900042
Maps: OS Landranger Sheet 165
            OS Explorer Sheet 2
            (or old Pathfinder Sheet 1118 (SP80/90))
            Chiltern Society FP Maps Nos. 3 & 8

How to get there/Parking: The Lee, 3 miles southeast of
Wendover, may be reached from the town by taking the
A413 towards Great Missenden for 1.4 miles, then turning
left onto a road signposted to Kingsash and The Lee. Follow
this winding lane for nearly two miles, then one-third of a
mile past 'The Gate', turn right at a crossroads and follow
a winding road for three-quarters of a mile to The Lee village
green. Cars may be parked along the road on the southern
(right-hand) side of the green which is not used by through
traffic, but should not block the road or driveways. Do not
use the pub car park without the landlord's permission.

The Lee is both a collective name for a group of isolated
hamlets and the particular name of one of them. Situated on a
hilltop plateau above the Misbourne valley and connected to
the outside world only by narrow winding lanes, The Lee
proper with its pub, manor house and a few cottages around
its pleasant village green, is a secluded haven of rural life. One
surprising feature of the village is that it has two churches.
The older one, of thirteenth-century origin, was replaced by
the nearby brick structure in 1868, but was retained as a
Sunday school and has since been restored. Both churches and
nearby Church Farm stand within the bounds of an ancient
camp, a circular earthwork, and this would suggest early
habitation of the area. In more recent times, the village manor
house was purchased in 1900 by Sir Arthur Lasenby Liberty,
the founder of Liberty's department store in London's Regent
Street, who proved a considerable benefactor to the village
and whose descendants still live locally.

The walk takes you first through the ancient camp between
the churches and Church Farm, then through open country
descending with fine views into the Misbourne valley at

WALK 4

Cock's Hill

Boswells
Barn
L11
Wood
W35
Concord
Wood
Great
Widmoor
Wood
L11

Lordling
Wood
L7
L Walk 5
11
KINGSASH
W
35 L45
L11
LEE
Walk 5
L19
Walk 5
GATE
'Old Swan'
L18b
L9
Walk
5
L18a
W40
SWAN
BOTTOM
WENDOVER
DEAN
W40
L18
W39
L16
Durham Farm
Wendoverdean Farm
King's
Lane
Old
L27 Plantation
Church
L48
Farm
Home
Bowwood Lane
L4
Farm
L4
L27
W37
THE LEE
Manor House
W L3
37
'Cock
& Rabbit'
Start

0   1 mile
0   1 kilometre

24

Wendover Dean. The heights are subsequently regained at Kingsash before you circle through a heavily wooded area on and above the Chiltern escarpment to reach Swan Bottom and return to The Lee.

Starting from the 'Cock and Rabbit' at The Lee village green, follow the side-road westwards around the southern side of the green. At the far end of the green, take the winding road out of the village past the new church. Just past the far end of the churchyard, turn left over a stile onto footpath L48. Follow a left-hand hedge concealing the old church to a gate and stile between Church Farm and a cottage. Here cross the stile, the drive to the cottage and a further stile and then take path L4 bearing half right across a field to a gate and stile. Cross the stile onto a track and, after a few yards, turn left onto a crossing track and follow a left-hand hedge for a third of a mile to a stile into King's Lane. Turn left onto this road and at a road junction, disregard Bowwood Lane branching to the right and turn right onto footpath L3, a track into a wood which runs parallel to Bowwood Lane. Where the track bears left away from the road, leave the track and follow the inside edge of the wood straight on beside the road to a gap into a field where wide views of the Misbourne valley open out ahead. Go through this gap and take path W37 following a right-hand hedge straight on downhill passing under a power line and through a hedge gap. After a third of a mile, on reaching what is normally a crop break extending a hedge line from the fields below, go through a gap in the right-hand hedge and join Bowwood Lane. Follow this road for a further third of a mile to a road junction just past Wendoverdean Farm.

Here go straight on along a 'no through road' following it round a sharp right-hand bend. At a second sharp right-hand bend, turn left into a hedged lane (footpath W39) and follow it winding uphill for some 250 yards. At a waymarked fork turn right through gates onto path W40 and follow a left-hand hedge, later a belt of trees. Beyond the belt of trees, where the hedge turns left, follow its winding course, gradually climbing to reach a stile at the far end of the field. Cross this stile onto path L9, then keeping just right of the bottom of the combe, continue straight on uphill heading towards a house to the right of one with large windows, to a stile which leads you into King's Lane near a road junction at Kingsash.

Turn left onto this road and at the road junction turn left again. After about 130 yards, by Robertswood Cottage, turn right into a rough lane (L45). Just past the cottage, leave the lane and take W35, a fenced path on the other side of the lane's left-hand hedge. Now follow this path through woodland for over half a mile, until it eventually drops down to rejoin the parallel bridleway (L45). Just beyond this, on reaching a track (L11, part of the Ridgeway Path), turn right onto it. At a fork, keep left following the Ridgeway Path waymarks, then, at a second fork, take the waymarked path forking right and follow it climbing steadily for a third of a mile. Where the path levels out, look out for a signposted path junction. Here turn right, leaving the Ridgeway but still on L11, onto a narrow woodland path which gradually swings to the left and reaches a crossing track. Turn left onto this track and at three subsequent forks, continue straight on ignoring a branching track to the left and two to the right. On emerging into a plantation, keep right following its right-hand edge, then, at its corner, continue straight on into mature woodland, ignoring two crossing tracks and bearing slightly right. Now go straight on through Great Widmoor Wood passing a triangulation post and ignoring several crossing tracks. On passing a field to your left, ignore a wide crossing bridleway known as Timberley Lane, then, where the track bears right and forks, take the left-hand option and follow its winding course through Lordling Wood for quarter of a mile. Just before reaching a rough road and some sheds, bear half left (crossing the route of Walk 5) onto a path through some holly bushes (still L11) which continues past the backs of several cottages to reach a squeeze stile by the corner of a field. Go through this squeeze stile and follow the right-hand hedge of an overgrown orchard, later diverging from the hedge and passing left of some cottages to reach a road some 130 yards north of the 'Old Swan'.

Turn right onto this road, then, almost immediately, turn left over a stile opposite the cottages onto footpath L19 and follow a right-hand hedge to a gate and stile. Cross this stile and continue to follow the right-hand hedge through two further paddocks to reach a gate and stile. Cross this stile and turn right onto L18b (joining Walk 5) following a right-hand hedge to a gate and stile. Having crossed the stile, take bridleway L18a along an old green lane straight on downhill (leaving Walk 5 again) to reach two bridle-gates leading onto a road in Swan Bottom.

Go through these gates, cross the road and take a gravel drive opposite (path L18). Ignoring a branch to the right, follow the drive to its end. Now follow a left-hand hedge straight on crossing four stiles until you enter a belt of trees. In the trees, turn left onto a track (L16) and follow it for some 200 yards to a fork. Here go right onto L27 and follow an obvious path through a wood called Old Plantation to a stile. Cross the stile and follow a right-hand hedge to a gate and stile. Having crossed the stile, bear half right up a hedged lane and past a converted barn to a further stile. Cross this and go straight on through a small copse past a pond to a road at The Lee where you turn right for the village green.

WALK 5: ✓   Cholesbury

Length of Walk: 7.3 miles / 11.8 Km

Starting Point: Cholesbury village hall.

Grid Ref: SP930071

Maps: OS Landranger Sheet 165
OS Explorer Sheet 2
(or old Pathfinder Sheet 1118 (SP80/90))
Chiltern Society FP Maps Nos. 3 & 8

How to get there/Parking: Cholesbury, 4 miles northwest of Chesham, may be reached from the town by taking the A416 northwards. At a sharp right-hand bend, leave the A416 and continue straight on along a road signposted to Cholesbury and Hawridge (not Bellingdon) and follow it for 3.7 miles to Cholesbury Common. The village hall is on the right about 150 yards past a turning signposted to Tring. Cars can be parked along the edge of the common.

Notes: Due, in part, to the remote nature of the area, some paths are in poor condition and difficult to follow. Also heavy nettle growth may be encountered in places in summer.

N.B Difficult in woods. X.
Maybe muddy. "

Cholesbury, with its cottages scattered around its spacious ridge-top common, is one of the most unspoilt villages in the Bucks Chilterns and forms the gateway to some of their most remote country. The village is also an ancient settlement, as its church, which is of thirteenth-century origin, but was largely rebuilt in 1872-3, stands within an Iron Age camp of sizeable proportions, being ten feet high and containing about fifteen acres of land.

The walk explores the remote, heavily-wooded hill country to the west of Cholesbury, skirting Lee Gate before descending the escarpment at The Hale, where there are superb views of the Wendover Gap. It then returns by a more northerly route, passing close to St. Leonards and Buckland Common. Despite the difficult conditions sometimes encountered, the walk is scenically most rewarding.

27

WALK 5

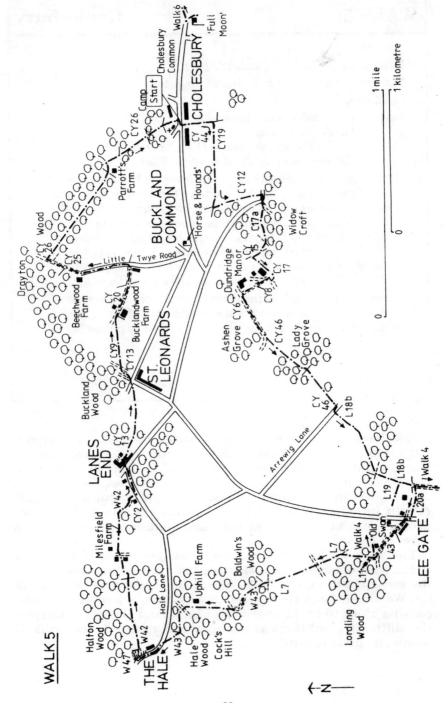

Starting from Cholesbury village hall, take the road westwards, then almost immediately turn left onto path CY44 left of the Old Rectory, taking a fenced path by the near end of a white fence to a stile. Cross this and follow a left-hand fence straight on downhill to a gate and stile in the bottom. Having crossed the stile, turn right onto path CY19 and follow a right-hand fence crossing two further stiles, then follow a right-hand hedge straight on through two fields to reach a tree belt at the far end of the second field. Here turn left onto path CY12, following the outside edge of the tree belt. Where, after some 30 yards, the tree belt bears away to the right, leave it, heading for the left-hand end of a row of tall poplars on the skyline to reach a road by the end of a hedge.

Turn right onto this road and at a sharp right-hand bend, leave it and take path CY17a, crossing a stile left of a private macadam road and joining the road just beyond the gates of a wood called Widow Croft. About 30 yards beyond the gates, fork right onto the second right-hand track. Where holly bushes block your way ahead, bear slightly right, ignoring a track to your left barred by sawn tree-trunks and continue to a rail-stile in the far corner of the wood. Cross this and take path CY15 beside a left-hand hedge for about 70 yards to a gap in it, then turn left through a gap and take path CY17 heading for the left-hand end of the buildings at Dundridge Manor. Go straight on past the buildings then bear half right to reach a concrete road (path CY8). Turn right onto this road, immediately bearing left and keeping left of the buildings, then continue past a large duckpond to your right, over a weighbridge and through some gates. Where the road turns right, leave it and turn left into a wide, ancient green lane (bridleway CY6), following it downhill to reach a wood called Ashen Grove. Where the lane bears right and enters the wood, leave it and take path CY46 straight on, following a left-hand hedge into a field. Here go straight on uphill to enter a wood called Lady Grove by a gap right of a tall ash tree, then follow an ill-defined path straight on through the wood, passing between a green shed and a shallow pit and descending to reach an obvious crossing path in the bottom. Cross this and continue straight on through a hedge gap into a field, then aim to pass just right of a clump of trees on the skyline to reach a hedge gap leading to Arrewig Lane.

Turn right onto this road and, after about 50 yards, turn left through a hedge gap onto path L18b, following a right-hand hedge downhill. Where three hedges meet in the valley bottom, go straight on through a gap between the other two and bear slightly right across the field, passing over a rise to reach a hedge gap with a waymarking post into a strip of woodland. In the wood, go straight on, crossing it diagonally to a stile. Cross this and follow a right-hand hedge uphill through two fields, joining the route of Walk 4. At the far side of the second field, cross a stile by a gate, then, after some 10 yards, turn right over the second right-hand stile onto path L20a (leaving Walk 4 again). Now follow a right-hand line of trees, later a fence to reach a gate and stile onto a road near the 'Old Swan'.

Turn right onto the road, then immediately left into a flint lane left of the pub (L43) and follow it until you enter Lordling Wood. Here turn right into the wood and take path L7, the central option of a three-way fork, recrossing the route of Walk 4 and following this waymarked path straight on through the wood. On emerging into a field, bear half left to cross a bridleway and sporadic hedge line just right of the bottom of a dip, then bear slightly right across the next field, with a wide view over your right shoulder towards Chesham, to reach a hedge gap right of a Scots pine into Baldwin's Wood.

In the wood, ignore a crossing path and take path W43 straight on into a plantation. Where the path forks, bear slightly left, soon passing between old brick gateposts into a field. Go straight on across the field to a hedge gap, then follow a grassy track through the corner of a wood and along its outside edge. Soon the track passes through another strip of woodland, where a pronounced section of the ancient earthwork known as Grim's Ditch is visible in the trees to your left. On emerging into another field, where the track turns right, leave it and go straight across the field to the right-hand end of a brick wall by a gate. Here pass through a V-stile and follow a fenced path around the wall of Uphill Farm. Where the path forks by another gate in the wall, take the right-hand option, following a right-hand hedge into Hale Wood and soon passing a redundant gate to reach the Ridgeway Path. Cross this and take a sunken path straight on downhill. At a crossways near the bottom edge of the wood bear half right ignoring a crossing path, then leave the wood crossing a stile and heading for a gate and signpost in the bottom corner of the field. Go through this gate and turn left into Hale Lane, passing the sixteenth-century Hale Farmhouse and Hale Barn at The Hale.

Just past Hale Barn, turn right onto bridleway W47. On entering Halton Wood, turn right onto path W42 up a flight of steps and over a stile, then turn left onto a track into a field. Now follow the outside edge of Halton Wood straight on until you reach a wooden pylon. Here bear slightly right, leaving the edge of the wood and walking under a powerline to a fence gap into another wood by the next pylon. Here turn round to admire the superb view towards The Hale and Bacombe Hill, before continuing steeply uphill through the wood under the powerline. Near the top of the hill, you recross the Ridgeway Path, leave the wood by a stile and turn left, following the outside edge of the wood, then a left-hand hedge to Milesfield Farm. Here go straight on between farm buildings, cross a concrete road and follow a left-hand hedge straight on to a hedge gap at the far side of the field. Go through this gap then, where the hedge turns left, keep straight on uphill to reach a concealed gate and stile in a corner of the field. Cross the stile and follow an old green lane straight on, soon with a garden fence to your right. Where the lane narrows to an enclosed path, take path CY2 along it bearing right to a road at Lanes End. Turn left onto the road and at a junction, pass the right-hand side of the grass triangle, cross the priority road and take the drive into Coppice Farm Park (path CY13). Now take the first turning right, then bear half left across a car park to a rail-stile. Now go straight on across a field to a stile left of the last mobile home. Cross this and go straight on, heading for a modern red-brick house right of the end of a wood ahead, to reach a hedge gap, then bear slightly left across the next field to a stile just left of the bottom corner of the field leading to a road junction on the edge of St. Leonards.

Now cross the road and a rail-stile by a gate opposite into Buckland Wood. Inside the wood, where the track forks, take the right-hand path along the inside edge of the wood, looking out for a stile out of the wood into a field. On reaching it, turn right over it onto path CY9, then bear half left across the field, heading for the left-hand barn at Bucklandwood Farm to reach the far corner of the field. Here bear half right onto a track (path CY20), going straight through the farm and continuing along a hedged lane to reach Little Twye Road on the edge of Buckland Common.

Turn left onto this macadam road and follow it to where it ends by a cottage. Here take a gravel lane (bridleway CY25) straight on, soon with Drayton Wood on your left, ignoring a stile and later a gate in the left-hand fence. Where the right-hand field ends, cross a stile in the right-hand fence onto path CY26 and follow its winding course along the inside edge of Drayton Wood for half a mile until you reach a stile to your right leading out of the wood. Ignore this stile and continue straight on, gradually bearing left until you reach a second right-hand stile. Turn right over this (still on CY26) and follow a right-hand hedge to a stile into another wood, then go straight on along the inside edge of this wood to a stile. Now follow an obvious path straight on through an area of scrub to a gap in the high banks and ditch of Cholesbury's Iron Age camp. Here cross the camp ditch and a stile by a gate and follow a slightly sunken track straight on across a field to cross a rail-stile by a gate between two oaks, then bear slightly right to a gate and stile. Cross the stile and follow a track straight on to reach Cholesbury Common by the side of the village hall.

Length of Walk: 7.9 miles / 12.8 Km
Starting Point: 'Full Moon', Hawridge Common
Grid Ref: SP935070
Maps: OS Landranger Sheet 165
            OS Explorer Sheet 2
            (or old Pathfinder Sheet 1118 (SP80/90))
            Chiltern Society FP Map No. 8
How to get there/Parking: Hawridge Common, 3.5 miles
northwest of Chesham, may be reached from the town by
taking the A416 northwards. At a sharp right-hand bend,
leave the A416 and continue straight on along a road
signposted to Cholesbury and Hawridge (not Bellingdon)
and follow it for 3.4 miles to the 'Full Moon' at Hawridge
Common, where cars can be parked along the edge of the
common.

Instructions difficult to follow
Muddy in woods

Hawridge (pronounced 'Harridge') and its neighbour
Cholesbury today form a long sporadic ribbon along a ridge
top road with most of their buildings on the south side and
their twin commons on the north side. Their boundary just
west of the 'Full Moon' can only be perceived by virtue of the
back-to-back nameboards marking it. The original site of
Hawridge village, which is visited in the course of the walk, is,
however, over a mile to the southeast of the 'Full Moon' and
consists of the church with its wooden bellcote built in 1856 to
replace a thirteenth-century building on the same site from
which the thirteenth-century font remains; timber-framed
Hawridge Court with its deep moat which has been filled in
front of the house and a former farm.

The walk explores the country to the south of Hawridge
with its succession of typical Chiltern ridges and bottoms and
visits the ridgetop villages of Bellingdon, Asheridge and
Chartridge. All these villages and the roads which serve them
are located on the ridges, as the valleys were formerly marshy.
Hence the paths used in this walk were vital means of
communication between the various ridges. Although the walk
is hilly, its scenery makes the effort well worthwhile.

Starting from the 'Full Moon' on Hawridge Common, cross the road and turn right along path 481 on the verge past a cottage. Just after its garden hedge ends, fork left onto a lesser path. By a pair of small oaks turn left onto an ill-defined path downhill. At a T-junction of paths turn right eventually dropping down to join a track along the bottom edge of the common (path CY48j). Now follow this track through an open heathland area for a third of a mile to reach a road. Turn right onto this road, then immediately left onto heathland path CY48f, soon bearing right at a fork and climbing, at one point ignoring a crossing path and later turning left then immediately right, to reach the top road opposite CY33, a signposted path right of 'Hill View'.

Take this path straight on through scrubland and on emerging into an open area, follow the left-hand hedge straight on to the corner of a fence. Here turn left onto path CY31 generally following the left-hand fence, later a hedge, eventually crossing a track and keeping left of a wooden shed. Now bear half right across a field to a stile. Cross the stile and another stile by a gate, then bear left and follow a left-hand hedge to a stile in the corner of the field. Having crossed this stile, ignore a stile to the left and follow a left hand fence straight on across a field to a gate and stile. Cross the stile and continue straight on between a hedge and a belt of trees, crossing a stile, the drive to Hawridge Place and another stile, until you pass through a kissing-gate into a sunken lane. Having crossed a stile opposite, continue straight on across a field following a left-hand fence, later a hedge to a gate and stile. Cross the stile and continue straight on past a former farm, at the far side of which path CY39 to your left enables you to make a detour to look at the church and Hawridge Court.

Otherwise, having briefly joined Herts. Walk 8 at the far end of the field by a copse concealing the deep moat of Hawridge Court, turn right onto path CY39 and follow a left-hand hedge downhill over a stile to a gate and stile. Cross the stile and bear half right across the corner of a field to a handgate by a cattle trough. Go through this, then turn left over high rails and follow a left-hand hedge downhill into a belt of trees. Here turn left over a stile on path CY30 and follow the belt of trees to a pair of right-hand stiles. Turn right over these and take path C34 following a right-hand fence uphill to a gap in the top hedge. Go through this and bear half left across a field (now on C36), passing the corner of a hedge to a gate and stile in the far corner of the field. Here turn right over the stile and follow a lane (C38a) into Bellingdon.

On reaching the main village road, turn right. After a few yards, turn left through a kissing-gate and follow path C48a beside a right-hand hedge to a hedge gap in the corner of the field. Here turn right through a kissing-gate onto path C47 following a right-hand hedge to a former gateway. Do not go through this, but turn left onto path C48 and follow a right-hand hedge downhill to a stile into Widmore Wood. Having crossed this, fork left then turn left onto a crossing track. Now turn immediately right and follow a path downhill to a crossing track in the valley bottom. Cross this track and bear half left uphill, joining one track, ignoring a crossing path and joining a further track until you leave the top of the wood by a concrete road. Follow this straight on to white gates at Widmore Farm, then bear half right passing right of the farmhouse to a road at Asheridge.

Turn right onto this road and after about 90 yards, turn left through a kissing-gate and follow path C19 beside a right-hand hedge downhill. Where the hedge turns right, leave it and continue straight on to a hedge gap on the other side of the valley, then follow a left-hand hedge straight on uphill. At the top corner of the field, continue straight on into a hedged path and follow it for quarter of a mile. On emerging into a field, follow the left-hand hedge, then a rough lane straight on to a road at Chartridge.

Turn right onto this road and after about 200 yards, turn left into Cogdells Lane. Follow this straight on to the end of its macadam, then continue straight on along a rough lane (C53). Where this lane forks, bear half right and where the lane turns right, go straight on over a stile by a gate and take path C6a following a left-hand hedge downhill to a stile in Pednor Bottom. Cross the stile and turn right onto bridleway C8 between a hedge and a fence, later a wood and a fence, and follow this along the bottom for quarter of a mile. Ignore a branching path into the right-hand wood. Where woodland begins to the left, turn right onto bridleway C9 along the inside edge of the right-hand woodland. After quarter of a mile, go straight on over a stile onto path C16a and follow it straight on for over half a mile through Hightree Wood and Lownde's Wood, disregarding all branching paths, until you leave the wood by a stile. Here take path L22 straight on across a field to a gate and stile, then follow a right-hand fence straight on to a stile onto a road near Lee Common.

Cross the stile, the road and a stile opposite into Grove Wood. Now bear half right and follow a waymarked path (L40) for about 140 yards to a waymarked crossways. Here turn right and follow waymarked path L21 to a road junction. Turn right onto the major road and follow it for about 250 yards. At the start of Bray's Wood to the left, turn left over a stile and bear half right following the ill-defined but waymarked path L25 across the wood to a stile leading out into a field. Now bear half left to the bottom corner of the field, then turn right and follow a left-hand hedge to a stile into Arrewig Lane at Threegates Bottom .

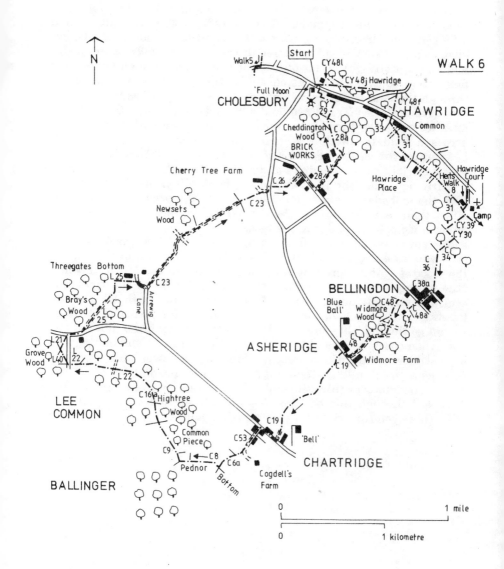

Cross the stile and turn right onto the road. At a right-hand bend, turn left and follow C23, a track beside a left-hand hedge, over a hill. Where the track transfers to the other side of the hedge, follow it. Near the top of the hill ignore a branching track to your right, then at a fork go right transferring back to the right-hand side of the hedge. Just past Newsets Wood, transfer to the left-hand side of the hedge and follow it straight on for quarter of a mile until you enter the next field. Here continue straight on across the field to a bridlegate. Go through this and continue straight on to cross a set of rails leading to the drive to Cherry Tree Farm and a road. Turn left onto the road and after a few yards, turn right over a stile and take path C26 straight across a field to another stile. Cross the stile and bear half left heading for the left-hand corner of a farm compound. Having crossed a stile here, join a concrete drive and follow it straight on out to a road.

Turn right onto the road and after about 200 yards, turn left onto C28, the macadam drive to a brickworks. At the brickworks, pass the office, then bear half right to the left-hand of two stiles. Cross this and follow a right-hand hedge to the back of the works, then turn left over a stile onto path C28a and follow a right-hand hedge, crossing another stile and entering Cheddington Wood. Now follow the inside edge of the wood downhill, ignoring a branching path to the left, to reach a stile at the bottom. Cross this stile, ignore a stile to the right and continue straight on to cross a further stile onto path CY29. Now follow a right-hand hedge uphill to a gate in the top corner of the field. Do not go through this, but turn left and follow a right-hand fence to a stile, then continue straight on to a stile in the right-hand hedge, with a good view ahead of Cholesbury Windmill, a tower mill originally built as a smock mill in 1863 but rebuilt in its present form in 1884. Now turn right over this stile and follow a fenced path to a small gate. Turn left through this and follow a right-hand hedge to a gate and stile where you turn right for your starting point.

WALK 7: Ashley Green

Length of Walk: 6.2 miles / 10.0 Km
Starting Point: Ashley Green village hall.
Grid Ref: SP977051
Maps: OS Landranger Sheet 165
        OS Explorer Sheet 2
        (or old Pathfinder Sheet 1118 (SP80/90))
        Chiltern Society FP Map No. 17
How to get there/Parking: Ashley Green, two miles
    south of Berkhamsted and two and a half miles north of
    Chesham, may be reached from either town by taking the
    A416 towards the other town. By Ashley Green Church,
    turn off the main road into Two Dells Lane signposted to
    Bovingdon and after 150 yards, turn left into the village
    hall car park.
Notes: Heavy nettle growth may be encountered in the
    summer in various places.

Despite its suburban appearance, Ashley Green, situated on a
hilltop plateau between the Chess and Bulbourne valleys is a
good centre for walking in the surrounding countryside. Much
of this walk is of an easy nature, exploring the upland plateau
to the east and south of Ashley Green and visiting Whelpley
Hill and Lye Green. In the latter stages of the walk, there is a
magnificent view of Chesham Vale and the hills beyond and
the walk takes you down into the Vale before reascending to
Ashley Green.

Starting from Ashley Green village hall, take Two Dells Lane beside
the green northwestwards to its crossroads with the A416 by Ashley
Green's neo-gothic Victorian church built in 1875. Turn right here
onto footpath AG7, a track which leads across and off the green to a
gate and stile. Cross the stile, then bear half right across a field to
another gate and stile. Having crossed this stile, follow a fenced path,
turning left then right, ignoring a stile in the left-hand fence and
crossing another stile at the far end of the right-hand field. Now follow
the left-hand hedge straight on. Where the hedge ends, turn right onto
a fenced track. On emerging into a field, go straight on over a hill to
an electricity pylon and stile in the hedge just beyond it. Cross this

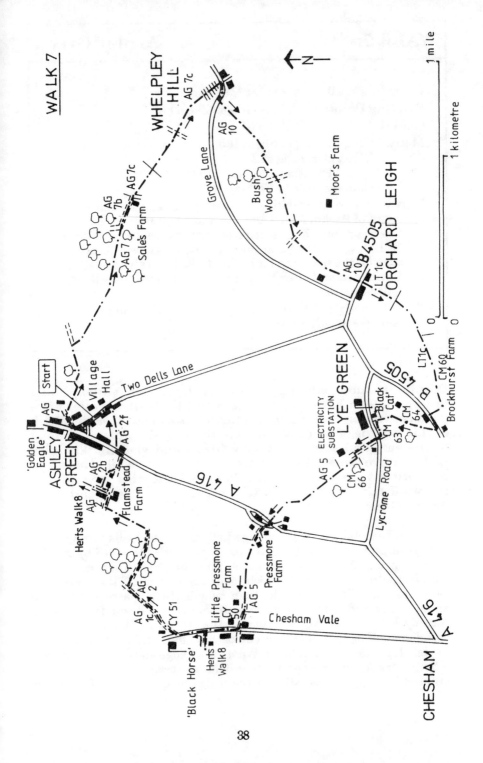

WALK 7

WHELPLEY HILL

AG 7c

AG 7b
AG7c
AG 7
Sales Farm

AG 10
Grove Lane

Bush Wood

Moor's Farm

ORCHARD LEIGH
B4505
AG 10
LT 1c
LT1c

CM 60
Brockhurst Farm

Two Dells Lane

Start
Village Hall

'Golden Eagle'
ASHLEY GREEN
AG 7
AG 2f

AG 2b
Flamstead Farm
Herts Walk8
AG 2

A 416

LYE GREEN
ELECTRICITY SUBSTATION
AG 5
B 4505
'Black Cat'
CM 64
CM 63
Lycrome Road

CM 66
AG 5

Little Pressmore Farm
AG 1c
CY 51
CY 50
AG 5
Pressmore Farm
Chesham Vale

'Black Horse'
Herts Walk8
AG 2

CHESHAM
A 416

N

1 mile
1 kilometre
0   0

38

stile and bear half left across a field, passing the right-hand end of a belt of trees, to a stile leading into a second belt of trees. Inside this belt of trees, take bridleway AG7b straight on uphill for some 200 yards to Sale's Farm. Here take path AG7c straight on between a hedge and a fence to a stile, then follow what is normally a crop break straight on for a third of a mile, ignoring a crossing path and eventually reaching a crossing track. Now cross this track, go straight on through a gap in the hedge and follow a left-hand fence straight on until you reach another hedge. Here follow a fenced path straight on through a caravan site crossing three site roads and eventually emerging at a road junction at Whelpley Hill.

Turn right here into Grove Lane and follow it round a sharp right-hand bend. Shortly after this bend, turn left over a stile onto footpath AG10 and follow what is normally a crop break across a field to the corner of a hedge. Here follow a left-hand hedge straight on. Where the hedge bears right, go through a gap in it and follow the other side of the hedge and later the outside edge of Bush Wood straight on to a hedge gap by the far end of this copse. Go through this gap, cross a bridleway and stile and continue straight on across a field to an electricity pole. Now bear slightly right to reach a stile by the corner of a hedge. Here cross another bridleway and the stile and continue straight on along what is normally a crop break to a point near the corner of a cottage garden where it bears slightly left and takes you to a gate and rails near two telegraph poles and a tree leading to the B4505 at Orchard Leigh.

Cross the rails and this road, then take footpath LT1c opposite between garden hedges. Follow this straight on, later between a hedge and a fence, until you emerge into a field. Bear slightly right across this field, on a line parallel to a right-hand hedge, to a stile in another hedge ahead. Cross this and a second stile and bear slightly right onto what is normally a crop break. Follow this for nearly a quarter of a mile to the end of a hedge. Here keep left of the hedge and follow it straight on. After about 250 yards, soon after the hedge bears slightly left, turn right through a gap in it (now on CM60) and follow a left-hand hedge to reach the B4505. Cross this road and turn left along its verge. Opposite the beginning of a barn at Brockhurst Farm, turn right though a hedge gap onto footpath CM64, then bear half right following a fenced path to another stile. Cross this and continue straight on across a field to the corner of a hedge left of a cottage. Here follow a right-hand hedge straight on, then, where the hedge turns right, bear slightly left along what is normally a crop-break to the corner of a hedge by a brick garage. Now keep straight on to a stile leading onto Lycrome Road at Lye Green near the 'Black Cat'. Do not cross this stile, but turn left onto path CM63, following a right-hand hedge crossing two wooden fences then turning right through a hedge gap onto Lycrome Road.

Cross this stile and Lycrome Road, then take a concrete drive (CM66) through gates opposite. At a second set of gates, turn left through a hedge, then turn immediately right into a hedged path (still CM66). Follow this straight on, disregarding a right-hand stile, until you emerge over a stile into a field (now on AG5). Here continue straight on across the field to the corner of a hedge, then bear slightly right and follow a left-hand hedge, later a fence, to a stile which leads you out to the A416.

Cross this road, bearing slightly left, and take a side-road opposite. After a few yards, turn left into the drive to Pressmore Farm (still AG5). Follow this straight on past the farm to two gates and stiles. Go straight on over the left-hand stile and follow a left-hand hedge straight on to another gate and stile. Having crossed this stile, continue to follow the left-hand hedge straight on to a further stile, where a magnificent view opens out across Chesham Vale. Cross this stile and follow a fenced path downhill passing left of a cottage, then ignoring a branching path to your left and taking path CY50 straight on downhill. On emerging through a gate onto a concrete farm road, follow it straight on downhill through Little Pressmore Farm, then continue over a stile to a road in Chesham Vale.

Turn right onto this and follow it for quarter of a mile to the 'Black Horse', joining the route of Herts. Walk 8. Opposite the pub, turn right onto bridleway CY51, a hedged lane and follow it (later becoming AG1c) winding uphill for quarter of a mile ignoring lesser branching tracks. Where the lane forks with a gate immediately ahead, turn right onto AG2 and follow this sunken lane winding uphill for a further quarter of a mile. Near the top of the hill the lane turns left and continues between hedges for 300 yards to reach a concrete farm road near Flamstead Farm. Turn right onto this, passing through a gate to reach a barn at the farm. By the barn, turn left to reach its far end, then, leaving Herts. Walk 8 again, turn right onto AG2b passing between farm buildings crossing a stile by a gate and continuing to a second gate and stile. Now go straight on past a shed and bear half right to a stile onto the farm drive. Turn left onto the drive and follow it to the A416 at the edge of Ashley Green.

Cross this road and turn left along its footway. After about 70 yards, turn right onto path AG2f between a hedge and a fence which leads you to a stile. Cross this and bear half right across a paddock to a gate and stile, then bear slightly left across a second paddock to two gates and stiles leading to a cul-de-sac road. Now continue straight on along this road to reach Two Dells Lane, then turn left onto it for the village hall.

WALK 8:   Ley Hill

Length of Walk: 6.6 miles/10.7 Km

Starting Point: 'The Crown', Ley Hill.

Grid Ref: SP990019

Maps: OS Landranger Sheets 165 & 166
OS Pathfinder Sheet 1119 (TL00/10) &
Explorer Sheet 2 (or old Pathfinder Sheet 1118 (SP80/90))
Chiltern Society FP Maps Nos. 5 & 17

How to get there/Parking: Ley Hill, 2 miles east of
Chesham, may be reached from the town by following the
signposted route from the northern end of the town centre
up White Hill and then turning right at a mini-roundabout
into Botley Road and continuing straight on for 1.4 miles.
At a multiple road junction near 'The Crown' and 'The
Swan', turn right and park either in a small car park on the
common on the left or in the loop road in front of the pubs.

Notes: This walk may be very muddy in wet weather.

Ley Hill, although connected to Chesham by a ribbon of
development along Botley Road, remains very much a typical
hilltop Chiltern hamlet with its pubs and cottages scattered
around its extensive common. Presumably as a result of
modern motor traffic, the common, which extends to the
Hertfordshire boundary, has long since ceased to be grazed by
sheep and so where it has not been converted for use as a golf
course or cricket field, scrubland and even woodland have
taken over.

The walk explores the hilltop plateau to the east of the
village, which, being capped with clay, has traditionally been
an area peppered with claypits and brickmaking activities.
Despite this and its close proximity to the built-up areas of
London and Watford, the plateau and the Hertfordshire
villages of Flaunden and Bovingdon, through which the walk
passes, retain a surprising feel of remoteness which totally
belies the fact of being a mere 20 miles from Central London.

Starting with your back to 'The Crown', cross the loop road and two
further roads across the common and turn right onto footpath LT15
crossing the village cricket field to reach a path through the trees just

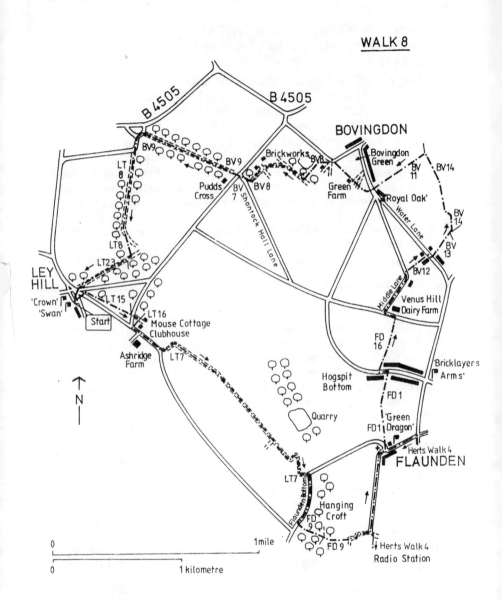

WALK 8

B 4505

B 4505

BOVINGDON

Bovingdon Green

BV9
BV 9
Brickworks BV8
BV 11
BV 14

LT 8
Pudds Cross
BV 7
BV 8
Green Farm
'Royal Oak'
BV 14

Shantock Hall Lane
Water Lane
BV 13

LT8
BV 12

LT23

LEY HILL
LT 15
Venus Hill Dairy Farm
Middle Lane

'Crown'
'Swan'
LT16
Mouse Cottage Clubhouse
Start
FD 16

Ashridge Farm
LT7
'Bricklayers Arm s'

Hogspit Bottom
FD 1

N

Quarry
'Green Dragon'
FD1

Herts Walk 4

FLAUNDEN

LT7
Flaunden Bottom
Hanging Croft
FD 9

0   1mile
0   1 kilometre

FD 9
Herts Walk 4 Radio Station

right of its far corner. Now take this path through the trees, pass left of a golfing green and follow the left-hand edge of a fairway. Where the fairway forks, keep left passing left of the 10th tee to reach a white gate. Here cross a road and take LT15 straight on along the macadam drive towards Mouse Cottage. By the cottage, turn right and follow path LT16 along the edge of the common to reach a road junction. Now turn left onto the road towards Latimer and Flaunden and follow it straight on, ignoring a turning to the right, until you reach a sharp right-hand bend. Here turn left through a bridlegate by double gates onto bridleway LT7, a track beside a right-hand fence which swings first left and then right and then continues straight along a lofty ridge. After a third of a mile the track begins to descend and joins a left-hand hedge. Ignore a gate in this hedge, then go through a gap by a gate and take a fenced track straight on winding downhill to reach a bend in the road marking the county boundary in Flaunden Bottom.

Turn right onto this road and follow it for quarter of a mile. Just before reaching a road junction, turn left onto FD9, a fenced bridleway leading uphill into a wood called Hanging Croft. Inside the wood, disregard a path branching right and continue straight on uphill to the top edge of the wood. Here ignore a branching bridleway to the right and follow a fenced bridleway straight on out of the wood heading towards a distant radio station. On reaching a wider fenced track, follow it straight on swinging left and then right until you reach a fork near the radio station. Here, joining the reverse direction of Herts. Walk 4, turn left onto a rough lane which leads you after nearly half a mile to the hilltop village of Flaunden.

Flaunden, locally pronounced 'Flarnden' is an unspoilt secluded village clustered around a crossroads of narrow lanes. Its brick and flint church with a bellcote, built in 1838 to replace a ruinous mediaeval structure in the Chess valley one and a half miles away, is notable for being the first to be designed by the celebrated architect Sir George Gilbert Scott. It incorporates several items from its predecessor including the one-handed church clock, the ancient church bells and the fifteenth-century font, allegedly once used as a nest for broody hens!

At the road junction by the church and School House, turn left, leaving Herts. Walk 4 again, and at a sharp left-hand bend, leave the road taking a fenced bridleway (FD1) straight on for a third of a mile to reach another road at the quaintly-named Hogspit Bottom. Here turn left onto the road and where the right-hand houses end, turn right over a stile onto FD16, a fenced path which after a quarter of a mile emerges over a stile onto another road at Venus Hill. Turn left onto this road passing Venus Hill Dairy Farm, then turn right into Middle Lane and follow it for quarter of a mile. After rounding a sharp left-hand bend, turn right over a stile onto path BV12 and take this fenced path to a stile by a barn. Cross this stile and go straight on between buildings to a road called Water Lane. Turn right onto this road, then almost immediately left over a stile by a gate onto BV13. Now follow a left-hand hedge to a gate and stile and then on to a further stile at the far end of the next field. Cross this stile, then turn left onto BV14 following a left-hand hedge which bears left at one point. Where the hedge turns left again, bear half right across the field to the corner of another hedge, then bear slightly left with the hedge to your right and continue to a stile in the corner of the field. Cross this stile and go straight on passing left of a holly tree to reach a further stile. Do not cross this, but instead turn left onto BV11 following a right-hand hedge through two fields. On crossing a stile into a third field, bear slightly left and follow a fenced path to reach a road at Bovingdon Green.

Here cross the road and continue to the back of the green, then turn right and follow the back of the green past Green Farm, one end of which is timbered, and the cricket pavilion. On emerging at a bend in Bovingdon Green Lane, turn left onto a macadam drive (path BV10). Where it forks, turn right over a stile onto BV8 and bear half left following a left-hand hedge to another stile. Having crossed this stile, turn left along a path between a hedge and an earth bank screening a claypit. On passing through a gap in a line of trees, turn right onto a track towards the brickworks. Just after the line of trees ends, fork left onto a fenced track past the brickworks. Near a green building, bear slightly left crossing another track and taking a further fenced track to reach a belt of trees at the edge of the works. Here turn right over a stile and follow a fenced path which ultimately leads you out to Shantock Hall Lane (BV7) near a road junction at Pudds Cross.

Turn right onto this road and at the junction, cross the major road and take BV9, a rough lane, straight on. Follow this lane, known as Pocketsdell Lane, straight on through a belt of trees for half a mile. Eventually you descend through a copse to a layby. Turn left into this then after 70 yards turn left between metal posts onto an old road. Where the road turns right, leave it and take bridleway LT8 known as Green Lane straight on. Now follow this lane straight on along the valley bottom and county boundary for over a third of a mile until you enter oak woodland on the edge of Ley Hill Common. About 40 yards into the wood, bear right at a fork and follow LT8 uphill through the woodland. On emerging at a crossing track, turn right and follow it (LT23) straight on, ignoring a branching path to the left and after a third of a mile reaching the road junction at Ley Hill opposite 'The Crown' and 'The Swan'.

WALK 9: ✓   Chesham

Length of Walk: 7.6 miles / 12.2 Km
Starting Point: 'Waggon & Horses', Chesham High Street.
Grid Ref: SP961019
Maps: OS Landranger Sheet 165
       OS Explorer Sheets 2 (or old Pathfinder Sheet 1118
       (SP80/90)) & 3 (or old Pathfinder Sheet 1138 (SU 89/99))
       Chiltern Society FP Maps Nos. 6 & 17
Parking: Car parks at Chesham Railway Station or in St.
   Mary's Way.
Notes: Heavy nettle growth may be encountered in the
   summer.

Chesham, set in a deep valley at the source of the River Chess, is an industrial town which has grown considerably during the past century. Traditionally a centre of the furniture, shoe and straw-plait trades, Chesham was the birthplace of Roger Crab, the seventeenth-century eccentric believed to be the inspiration for the 'Mad Hatter' in Lewis Carroll's 'Alice in Wonderland'. The town's expansion came with the arrival of the Metropolitan Railway in 1889 which brought with it the inter-war 'Metroland' phenomenon of residential expansion in rural areas suitable for daily commuting into London. Despite this, the old part of the town around Church Street, where the source of the Chess, some quaint old cottages and the twelfth- to fourteenth-century church are situated, is well worth a visit.

The walk, which soon leaves the urban area behind, is rewarding as it follows the northern slopes of the Chess valley to the outskirts of Latimer with fine views of this beautiful valley in places. The return over the hills to the north of this passes through surprisingly remote open country and culminates in a fine view of Chesham and the hills to the west before a rapid drop into the town centre.

Starting from the 'Waggon and Horses' at the northern end of the High Street, cross the High Street and take a road called White Hill opposite. After about 70 yards, turn right between bollards into The Backs, soon joining a road and following it to the railway station.

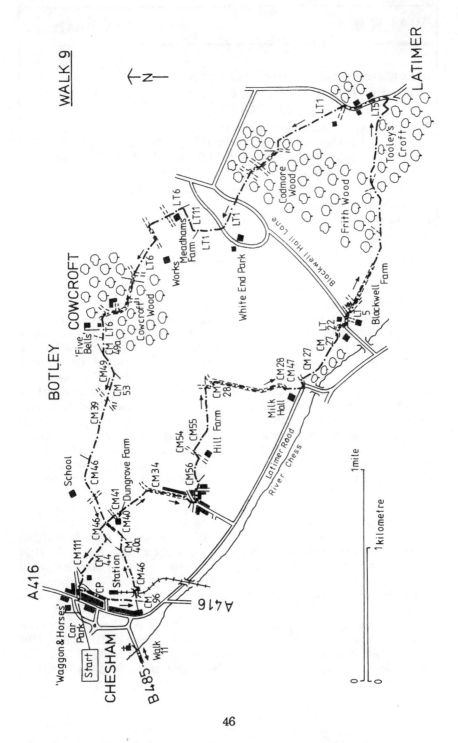

WALK 9

Where the road turns right here, take a fenced macadam path (CM96), straight on beside the railway. Just past the end of the station platform, turn left over a railway bridge onto path CM46, then at the far end of the bridge turn right. After about 40 yards, turn sharp left up a couple of steps and follow a fenced terraced path which soon turns right and climbs more steeply eventually emerging over two stiles into a field. Here go straight on across the field, aiming for the left-hand end of Dungrove Farm when it comes into view, to reach a stile. Cross this and take path CM40a straight across the next field, aiming for a tall oak tree right of the farm, to reach another stile. Do not cross this, but turn left onto path CM40 following a right-hand fence to a stile. Now follow the left-hand fence past the farm crossing a further stile to reach two stiles by a New Zealand (barbed-wire) gate. Cross the right-hand stile and turn right onto path CM41 following a right-hand fence to a gate and stile onto a track into the farm. Here follow a right-hand hedge straight on through two fields to reach CM34, an old green lane known as Trapp's Lane. Turn right into this lane and follow it for quarter of a mile to emerge through an anti-motorcycle barrier into Rose Drive on the outskirts of Chesham.

At a crossroads ahead, turn left into Larks Rise and where this road turns right, take path CM56 straight on between a hedge and a fence to a kissing-gate into a field. In the field, bear slightly left and follow a left-hand hedge to a stile in the far corner. Cross this and turn left into a lane (CM54). After a few yards, turn right over a stile onto path CM55 and bear slightly left across a field passing left of two oaks to a stile at the corner of a hedge. Cross this stile and follow a left-hand hedge downhill through two fields, crossing a stile between these fields. At the bottom of the second, cross another stile and turn right onto CM28, a hedged lane called Bottom Lane. At a junction of lanes, turn right and follow Bottom Lane for over a third of a mile until you emerge through a bridlegate into a field. Bear half left onto a stony track across the field to a gate onto Latimer Road left of Milk Hall. Turn left onto this road and at a right-hand bend turn left into a hedged lane (CM47), then immediately right over a stile onto path CM27 into a field. Follow a line of trees straight across the field with the Chess not far to the right, to two more stiles. Cross these and bear slightly left along what is normally a worn path to a stile, then continue through a narrow paddock to a gate and stile. Having crossed the stile, take path LT22 following a right-hand garden wall and soon joining a macadam drive which bears right by a cottage to reach Blackwell Hall Lane.

Turn left onto this road and at a left-hand bend, where there is a fine view to your right of the fifteenth-century timber-framed Blackwell Farm with its jutting upper storey, go straight on along a rough drive (LT5). Where the drive forks, keep right through a gate. At the far end of a left-hand barn, keep right at a fork to cross a stile by a gate. Now follow a right-hand hedge straight on through three fields, passing through gates at the dividing fences, to a small gate into scrubland. Go through the gate and the scrubland, then bear left and follow a fenced path along the edge of Frith Wood uphill for quarter of a mile ignoring a branching path into the wood. At the top of the hill, follow the path bearing half left into woodland and continue straight on, disregarding all branching paths, until you emerge in the corner of a field.

Here bear half right and follow the outside edge of the wood for over a third of a mile to the far end of the field, then turn left and follow the right-hand fence to a stile in it. Turn right over this and follow the remains of a concrete path to a stile onto a road on the outskirts of Latimer.

The village, which is to the right, has no pub, but is still worth a visit. Formerly known as 'Isenhampstead Latimer', it was for centuries the property of the Cavendish family (later the Lords Chesham). During a prosperous period of the nineteenth century, Latimer House, the former seat of the Cavendish family, the church (designed by the celebrated architect Sir George Gilbert Scott in 1841) and much of the village were systematically rebuilt and the result is a much admired picture-book Chiltern village.

If not visiting the village, turn left along the road and follow it for quarter of a mile. At the far end of a left-hand copse, at a right-hand bend, turn left through a gateway onto a track, then immediately bear half right onto path LT1 across a huge field. After just over a third of a mile, cross a stile into Codmore Wood just left of a kink in its edge. In the wood you soon join a track and follow it straight on through this bluebell wood, disregarding a branching path to your right. On reaching a large clearing, bear slightly left along its left-hand edge crossing a major track and taking a grassy track straight on. Where the track ends at a crossing track, continue straight on through the trees to a stile which leads you out of the wood. Go straight on across the field to a stile leading onto Blackwell Hall Lane.

Cross this road and a stile opposite and follow a left-hand fence straight on, with White End Park with its palmhouse to your left, to reach gates and a stile onto another road. Cross this road and take a path opposite between a hedge and a fence. Ignore a stile in the left-hand fence and take path LT11 straight on, soon turning right, passing a house and eventually emerging over a stile into a field. Here turn left onto path LT6 following a left-hand fence to a stile onto a drive. Cross the stile, the drive and a further stile and continue straight on across two fields to a stile leading onto a rough road. Turn left onto this road (still LT6) and after about 90 yards, turn right through a hedge gap. Now bear half left across a field to a fence gap by Cowcroft Wood. Go through this gap and bear half left onto a track into the wood. Follow this track straight on, disregarding all crossing and branching tracks and on leaving the wood continue past Cowcroft Farm until you reach a fork with a raised triangular island near the hamlet of Cowcroft.

Here bear half left towards Cowcroft, then turn immediately left over a stile (still on LT6). In the field, turn right and follow its right-hand boundary past the hamlet. Ignore a gate and stile in the right-hand fence, then go through a handgate onto path CM49 and continue to follow the fence to an old gateway. Go through this gap, then bear half left and follow a track beside a left-hand hedge. At the end of the hedge, turn right onto CM53 following what is normally a crop-break, joining a sporadic right-hand hedge and following it downhill to Bottom Lane. Having crossed this lane and a stile, take path CM39 bearing half left uphill to a pair of stiles. Cross these and bear half right across a field to a hedge gap in its far corner. Go through this and take path CM46 following a right-hand hedge until you reach a crossing track. Cross this track and a stile opposite and continue straight on across a field to two stiles right of Dungrove Farm. Having crossed both these stiles, follow a fenced track to the far side of the left-hand field, then turn left over a stile and follow a right-hand hedge. After a further 100 yards, where the hedge bears slightly left, turn right over a stile onto CM44 and head for an oak tree ahead. Now continue straight on downhill with panoramic views across Chesham ahead to reach a stile. Cross this and continue straight on downhill to a further stile leading to a macadam path (CM111). Turn left onto this and follow it, swinging right, until it joins White Hill, then continue straight on for the town centre.

WALK 10: ✓   Amersham (South)

ɔk

Length of Walk: 5.7 miles / 9.1 Km
Starting Point: Broadway Car Park, Old Amersham.
Grid Ref: SU960972
Maps: OS Landranger Sheet 176 or Sheets 165 & 175
     OS Explorer Sheet 3
     (or old Pathfinder Sheet 1138 (SU89/99))
     Chiltern Society FP Map No. 6
Parking: A good car park is available on the north side
of the Broadway in Old Amersham or on-street parking
is possible in the High Street.

Amersham, in mediaeval times a borough known as 'Agmondesham' famous for its religious dissidents and martyrs including Lollards and later Quakers, has today one of the best preserved traditional High Streets of any Chiltern town. Most of its buildings date from the sixteenth to eighteenth centuries, while several are, at least in part, of fifteenth-century origin. The Market Hall, which protrudes into the High Street, was built in 1682 by Sir William Drake of nearby Shardeloes. Amersham church, of thirteenth-century origin but later extensively altered, contains numerous interesting monuments, including many to the Drake family, and is where the Coleshill-born poet, Edmund Waller, was christened in 1606. Sixteenth-century Bury Farm, at the foot of Gore Hill, is also of historical interest, as the leading Quaker, Mary Penington, took refuge there in 1666 during her husband's imprisonment.

The walk traverses some fine open hill country south of the town between Coleshill and Chalfont St. Giles and there are extensive views, particularly in the latter stages of the walk.

Starting from the entrance to the car park, follow the road eastwards to the roundabout at the foot of Gore Hill (A355). Turn right onto the A355 and follow it past Bury Farm to a roundabout on the bypass. Here turn right onto a macadam path (A23) climbing to the end of a footbridge over the bypass, then turn left onto path A23c over this bridge. At its far end, follow the path straight on to reach the back fence of gardens, then turn right onto fenced path A22 behind the gardens. On leaving the houses behind, take a grass track straight on up the valley for a third of a mile. Just before an ash tree (the first tree along the track), turn sharp right into the next field (now on path A21) and head for the right-hand corner of the field. Now turn sharp left onto path A24, following a right-hand grass bank to the third in a line of oak trees. Here bear half left across the field to a gap left of a wooden shed by a cottage. Now follow a hedged path (CO16) straight on uphill to a bend in a road on the edge of Coleshill.

Turn right onto the road and follow it to a sharp right-hand bend. Here go straight on, leaving the road and crossing a stile between gates onto path CO1. Now follow the left-hand hedge straight on through three fields. At the far end of the third field, cross two stiles, then bear half left still following the left-hand hedge. Where the hedge turns left again, leave it and bear half right following what is usually a crop-break over a rise towards tall bushes ahead. At the far side of the field, turn left onto path CO2 and keeping left of a hedge, follow it to the far end of the field. Here bear slightly right through a gap in the fence and hedge, then cross a footbridge and climb some rough steps to the A355.

Cross this road bearing slightly left to cross a stile virtually opposite, then follow a right-hand hedge (still on CO2) for quarter of a mile to a gate in the right-hand hedge. Turn right through this then left to cross a stile. Now bear slightly right through a plantation to cross a stile, then bear slightly left through an area of scrub to a stile right of a cottage. Cross this and the cottage drive, then follow a left-hand hedge straight on to another stile. Having crossed this, continue straight on across the next field, joining a left-hand hedge after crossing a slight dip and following it to a hedge gap into the next field. Now follow a left-hand hedge to a stile in it, then continue on the other side of the hedge to a stile leading into the sunken Bottom House Farm Lane. On the other side of the road, climb a couple of steps to cross a stile onto path CG47, then follow a left-hand fence uphill, with extensive views towards the Misbourne valley to your left, to reach a redundant stile. Here go straight on crossing two dips, heading for a small oak tree right of a red-tiled roof on the skyline to reach a redundant stile, then bear slightly right to a stile in a hedge gap right of an ash tree. Now cross this stile and take a grassy track straight on to a stile leading to a bend in a rough lane, with a view ahead towards the Chalfonts and London.

Turn left into this lane (CG46) and follow it, winding downhill for nearly half a mile, disregarding two branching tracks and joining CG28, to reach Bottom House Farm Lane at Upper Bottom House Farm. Turn right onto this road then, at the far end of the left-hand silage clamp, turn left onto path A18 along a concrete farm road to a flight of steps and stile leading into a field. Now follow a left-hand fence uphill to cross a stile, then, keeping right of a fence ahead, gradually diverge from it to reach a stile left of an electricity pylon. Cross this and bear half right across the next field, heading just left of the left-hand end of Day's Wood ahead and crossing a fenceline to reach a gate and stile in the far corner of the second field. (NB If there is no stile in the first fenceline, use the stile in the right-hand corner of the field.) Here cross the stile and, with fine views across the Misbourne valley to your right, follow the left-hand hedge for some 350 yards. Where the hedge turns left, continue straight on across the field to the corner of a hedge, then go straight on across a further field to a stile into Rodger's Wood. Inside the wood, follow an obvious path to a stile. Cross this and bear half left across a field, heading left of a large green factory building in Amersham, to a hedge gap. Now continue straight on across the next field to a gate and stile right of the far corner. Cross the stile and turn left onto a track leading through an underpass under the A413 to a cattle grid, gate and stile at Bury Farm. Having crossed the stile, follow a farm road, bearing right to a gate and stile onto Amersham Broadway, where a left turn returns you to your point of departure.

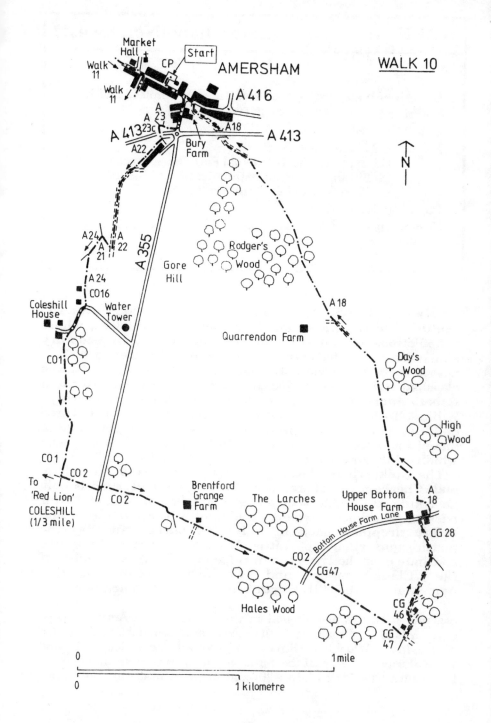

WALK 10

WALK 11:   Amersham (Northwest)

Length of Walk: 10.6 miles / 17.0 Km or 10.8 miles / 17.4 Km
Starting Point: Market Hall, Old Amersham.
Grid Ref: SU958973
Maps: OS Landranger Sheet 165
       OS Explorer Sheets 2 (or old Pathfinder Sheet 1118
       (SP80/90)) & 3 (or old Pathfinder Sheet 1138 (SU89/99))
       Chiltern Society FP Maps Nos. 6 & 8
Parking: See Walk 10.
Notes: Heavy nettle growth may be encountered in places in
the summer months.

Amersham, described in Walk 10, has owed much over the
centuries to the Drake family of nearby Shardeloes, whose
benefactions to the town include the seventeenth-century
almshouses and the market hall. Shardeloes itself, which is
passed early in the walk, was built for the Drake Family in the
classical style between 1758 and 1766 by Stiff Leadbetter and
Robert Adam. The house previously on this site was where
William Tothill, who is reputed to have fathered thirty-three
children, entertained Elizabeth I and it was the marriage of
one of his daughters to Francis Drake of Esher in about 1605
which established the Drake family at Shardeloes.

The walk, which, despite visiting the towns of Amersham
and Chesham, is characterised by open and surprisingly
peaceful countryside, soon leaves Amersham behind and after
passing Shardeloes, explores the quiet hills around Mop End
before dropping back into the Misbourne valley at the
picturesque village of Little Missenden. From there you
continue over the Hyde Heath ridge into the upper reaches of
the Chess valley and Chesham, before skirting
Amersham-on-the-Hill on your way back to Old Amersham.

Starting from the market hall in the centre of Old Amersham, go
eastwards along Broadway to the second mini-roundabout, then turn
right into Whielden Street (signposted to 'Hospital' and
'Crematorium'). Just past the 'Saracens Head', turn right into a rough
lane called The Platt (path A26) and follow it past some attractive

cottages and uphill to the gates of the cemetery. Here take an enclosed path right of the cemetery gates straight on and follow it to Cherry Lane. Cross this road and cross a stile opposite (still on A26), then take a fenced path along the bottom edge of the field to reach a kissing-gate. Go through this and continue straight on, soon reaching a stile onto the A413 Amersham Bypass. Cross the stile and the bypass, then cross a stile opposite. Now bear half right and follow a right-hand hedge to reach a crossing track. Here take path A27 bearing slightly left across a large field heading towards the chimneys of Shardeloes. At the top of a rise, the house comes into full view ahead, then go straight on, still heading for Shardeloes, to a kissing-gate in a corner of the field leading onto its drive. Turn left onto the drive, then immediately left again through a second kissing-gate and follow a left-hand hedge then a sporadic belt of trees and later a track along the outside edge of Wheatley Wood for half a mile. At the far end of the wood, where the track turns left, go straight on following a left-hand hedge to reach the edge of another wood called The Rough Park. Here turn right then left through a fence gap and over a stile and bear right then left following a left-hand fence at first. Now continue straight on for quarter of a mile through scrubby woodland until a fence ahead forces you to turn left. Here follow a left-hand fence at first, passing under a power-line and reaching a large pylon. Just beyond this pylon, fork right and follow an obvious path along the inside edge of the wood for quarter of a mile to reach a road at the hamlet of Mop End.

Turn right onto this road, then, at a sharp right-hand bend, leave it crossing a concealed stile right of gates ahead and taking path LM13 bearing left across a field to a stile at the point where a fenced track lined with young trees goes through a gap in a mature hedge. Cross this stile then turn right and follow a grassy track beside a right-hand hedge. At the far end of the field, cross a stile by a gate and bear half left across a field to a hedge gap just left of the far corner, then continue straight on across the next field to the corner of a hedge, where a rail stile leads you into Toby's Lane. Turn right into this lane (LM26) and follow it for a third of a mile passing through Breaches Wood. Some 200 yards beyond the wood, turn left over a stile onto path LM14 and bear half right passing just right of a twin-trunked ash tree to reach a stile by double gates leading to a road junction on the edge of Little Missenden. Here turn right into the village and at a junction by the sixteenth-century Manor House, turn left. The Manor House was, at one time, the home of Dr Benjamin Bates, physician to Sir Francis Dashwood and one of the notorious 'Knights of St. Francis', but, despite their alleged orgiastic life-style which he always denied, Dr Bates lived to be 98! The church, next to the Manor House, is of tenth-century origin and thus one of the oldest in the Chilterns. Its chancel arch contains Roman bricks and it can also boast twelfth- to fourteenth-century murals of St. Christopher and St. Catherine which were only rediscovered in 1931.

After passing the church, turn right over a stile by double gates onto path LM17, following the churchyard wall, then a belt of trees, crossing a footbridge over the River Misbourne and reaching a stile onto the A413. Cross the stile, this fast main road and a stile opposite, then continue straight on to a handgate between electricity poles leading to a footbridge over the Marylebone – Aylesbury railway line. At the far end of the footbridge, go straight on to a T-junction of paths, then turn left passing a gate and bearing half right onto a well-worn path (still LM17) along the inside edge of Mantle's Wood. After quarter of a mile, by Mantle's Farm to your right, ignore a crossing track and continue straight on, now on a cart-track, until you eventually enter a clear-felled area. At the far end of this, ignore another crossing track and follow a grassy track for quarter of a mile leaving the wood and following a right-hand hedge to reach a road at Hyde Heath.

Turn right along the roadside verge, then at a slight left-hand bend, turn left crossing the road and taking bridleway LM34, a stone track, after 15 yards forking right onto a woodland path. By a marker post near a cottage to your left, turn right, immediately forking left. After some 350 yards, on reaching a T-junction with a flint lane (bridleway LM33), turn left into it and follow it straight on (soon bridleway C2) to where it ends at white gates. Now go through a gap by these gates and take path C3 straight on along a flint track, later a concrete road, for a third of a mile to reach Hawthorn Farm. Here cross a stile by gates and turn right onto path C3a, a fenced concrete farm road. Follow this, turning right then left and continuing along a flint track beside a left-hand hedge with views towards Chesham starting to open out to your left. After passing a left-hand copse, the track turns right into White's Wood and Chesham Church comes into view ahead. Here leave the track and follow the outside edge of the wood, later a right-hand hedge straight on for quarter of a mile. About 100 yards short of the bottom corner of the field, turn right over a concealed stile onto path CM10 and bear half left across a field to gates in the bottom corner left of a bungalow. Go through these, turn right onto a macadam path beside the B485 and follow it for three-quarters of a mile into Chesham.

By the 'Queen's Head', if wishing to look at the picturesque cottages in Church Street and visit the twelfth- to fourteenth-century church, take Church Street straight on and by No.70, cross the road and take a fenced, cobbled path (CM2) up through a green gate to reach the

WALK 11

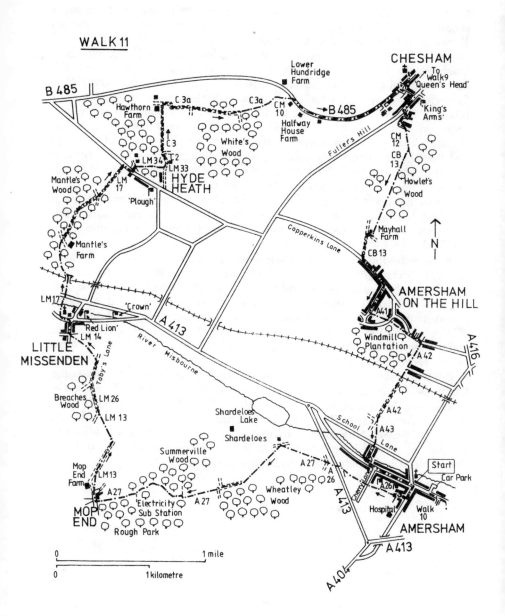

church. Otherwise, turn right by the 'Queen's Head' into Wey Lane, then, after some 200 yards, turn right up Fuller's Hill. On reaching a green to the left, turn left then right into Fuller's Close. At a second T-junction, turn right again and follow a road round the back of some bungalows until you reach signposted footpath CM12 through a kissing-gate to your right. Go through this gate and bear half left across a field to a gate and stile. Cross the stile and take path CB13 following a right-hand hedge at first and then bearing slightly left heading for two tall chestnut trees on the skyline to reach a kissing-gate, where there are fine views over Chesham behind you. Go through this gate and continue straight on to the corner of a hedge right of the chestnut trees. Here go straight on with a hedge first to your left then to your right until you reach a concrete yard at Mayhall Farm, then continue straight on crossing two stiles and passing between hedges to emerge into a field. Now turn right onto a track (still CB13) into another farmyard, then turn left along a macadam drive to reach Copperkins Lane on the outskirts of Amersham-on-the-Hill.

Turn left along this road, then after nearly quarter of a mile by a postbox, turn right into Weedon Lane. Just before the road turns left, turn left into a narrow hedged lane (path A41) which soon crosses a road. Now continue straight on, ignoring a stile into a wood, crossing the ends of two roads and passing a recreation ground. At the far end of the recreation ground, where the path widens into a road, turn right through a hedge gap onto path A42 and follow it along the edge of the recreation ground. At its far side, continue straight on through woodland past the end of a road to reach a railway level-crossing. Cross this and take a fenced path downhill. After a third of a mile, where the left-hand fence bears left, follow it (now on path A43) heading for a tall building at Amersham Hospital to reach a hedge gap. Go through this, then continue straight on through scrubland to emerge at a road junction. Here take Mill Lane straight on to reach the High Street, then turn left for your starting point.

WALK 12: ✓   Great Missenden

Length of Walk: 7.5 miles / 12.0 Km

Starting Point: Great Missenden Post Office at the junction of the A4128 and the High Street.

Grid Ref: SP894014

Maps: OS Landranger Sheet 165
OS Explorer Sheet 2
(or old Pathfinder Sheet 1118 (SP80/90))
Chiltern Society FP Map No.8

How to get there/Parking: Great Missenden, 4.7 miles northwest of Amersham, may be reached from the town by following the A413 to the twin roundabouts at its junction with the B485 and A4128. At the second roundabout, turn left onto the A4128, where, after 200 yards, there is a car park on the right.

muddy in places

Great Missenden, near the source of the fitful River Misbourne, has a long, narrow, picturesque High Street flanked by a number of old coaching inns, cottages and small shops, typical of a small town astride an old turnpike road. Apparently there were many more coaching inns in the past, but the arrival of the Metropolitan Railway in 1892 led to a loss of trade. Thanks to the town's bypass, which was controversial when it was constructed because it sliced through Abbey Park and cut the church off from the town, it is possible fully to appreciate the High Street's old world charm. The fourteenth-century church, which you pass in the early part of the walk, stands in a prominent hillside location on the edge of the Abbey Park. The Abbey itself, which was founded by William de Missenden in 1133 and was in the Middle Ages one of the largest in the county, has recently had to be rebuilt following a disastrous fire which gutted it.

The walk soon leaves Great Missenden and the Misbourne valley behind and explores the quiet hilltop plateau to the east separating the Misbourne valley from the heads of some of the various Chiltern 'bottoms' which meet at Chesham to form the Chess valley, visiting or skirting the hamlets of Hyde End, South Heath, Ballinger and Potter Row, before descending with fine views back into the Misbourne valley.

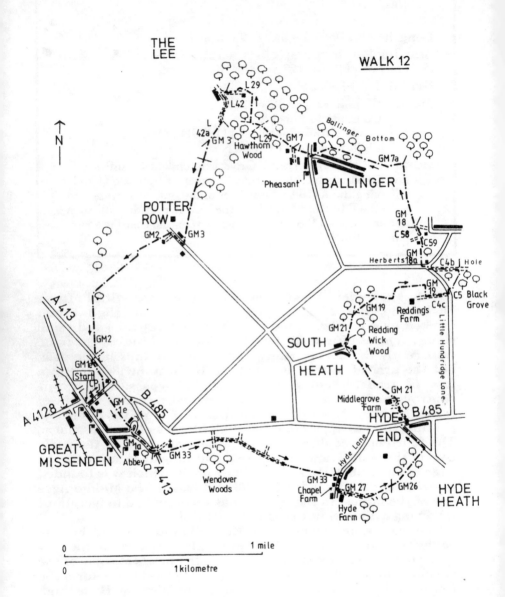

THE LEE

WALK 12

BALLINGER

POTTER ROW

Hawthorn Wood

'Pheasant'

Ballinger Bottom

GM 18
C 58
C 59
GM 18a
Herberts
C4b Hole

GM 19
C5 Black Grove
C4c

GM 19
Redding's Farm
GM 21
Redding Wick Wood

SOUTH

HEAT

Little Hundridge Lane

GM 21
Middlegrove Farm

HYDE

B485

END

A 413

GM2

GM1e
Start

A 4128

B 485

GREAT
MISSENDEN

GM 1a
Abbey

A 413

Wendover
Woods

Hyde Lane

GM 33

Chapel
Farm

GM 27

GM26

HYDE
HEATH

Hyde
Farm

0   1 mile

0   1 kilometre

60

Starting from the Post Office at the junction of the A4128 and the High Street, take the right-hand pavement of the A4128 northeastwards. On reaching the entrance to Buryfield Car Park, turn right onto path GM1e through the car park to reach the corner of a hedge. Here take a macadam path straight on beside the left-hand hedge. At the far end of the recreation ground, go straight on through a hedge gap into a rough lane and follow it to reach a road by a small green. Turn right along the edge of this green to a road junction at the end of the green, then turn left onto path GM1a, a narrow road leading to the church. Follow this road uphill for some 250 yards and over the bypass bridge into the churchyard. Here leave the drive and bear half right onto path GM33 across the churchyard, passing right of the church to reach a kissing-gate under a large lime tree. Go through this gate into Abbey Park, then turn left, heading for two stiles flanking a lane left of a pylon on the skyline. Cross these stiles and the lane and bear slightly right across a field, following the vestiges of a track over the skyline to two gates and a stile. Having crossed the stile, continue to follow the track, now beside a left-hand hedge. Ignore a gate in the hedge and when the track peters out, follow the hedge straight on to reach a stile in a corner of the field. Cross this and follow a right-hand hedge through two field. In the second field, look out for a stile in the right-hand hedge. On reaching it, cross it and follow a path between hedges to Hyde Lane.

Turn right onto this road and follow it past Chapel Farm, then, before reaching Hyde Farm, turn left onto path GM27, a concrete farm road, going straight on past the farm and descending into the valley bottom. Where the concrete road turns right just before its surface ends, leave it, crossing a stile by a gate and continue straight on, passing left of a copse concealing an old gravel pit, to reach a stile on path GM26 into the end of a tree-belt. Cross this stile and follow a path straight on through the tree-belt, which, in May, is profuse with bluebells, to reach the Hyde Heath road. Turn left onto this road and at its junction with the B485 at Hyde End, turn right, then almost immediately left, crossing the main road and taking path GM21, a macadam private road with a cattle grid. Where this road turns left into Middlegrove Farm, bear slightly right leaving the road to reach a stile. Cross this and bear slightly left, joining a track and passing between farm buildings. Where the track forks, go straight on over a rail-stile left of two gates, then bear half left across a field to a stile in the far corner. Cross this and follow a left-hand hedge climbing gently. Just before reaching the far end of the field, turn left over a stile into a fenced path and follow it to a stile leading to a rough lane at South Heath.

Follow this lane straight on to where it becomes a macadam road, then about 20 yards further on, turn right through a gate into a green

61

lane leading into Redding Wick Wood. On entering the wood, ignore a branching path to the right and continue straight on along the inside edge of the wood for some 200 yards, until you reach a crossing path. Here turn right onto path GM19 and after a few yards, where this forks, take the left-hand option straight on, passing just left of moated earthworks (which the name of the wood suggests to be the site of a lost village) and continuing straight on across the wood to a stile at its far corner. Cross this stile and follow a right-hand hedge straight on to a gate. Do not go through the gate, but instead turn left and follow a right-hand fence to a stile. Cross this and go straight on, then, where the fence turns right, follow it, wiggling to the left at one point, then, where it turns right again, follow it again to reach the drive to Redding's Farm. Turn left onto the drive and follow it (later on path C4c) to Little Hundridge Lane.

Turn left onto this road, then, almost immediately, turn right onto path C5 through a gap by wooden rails into a wood called Black Grove. Now follow a path descending to reach a fenced bridleway in the valley bottom called Herbert's Hole. Turn left onto this bridleway (C4b) and follow it to reach a road junction by a cottage. Here go straight on past the cottage, then, at the far end of its garden, turn right over a stile by a gate onto path GM18a, following a fenced path uphill, ignoring a stile into a wood. At the top corner of the left-hand field cross a stile and take fenced path C59 to a stile onto a gravel drive by a cottage. Take this drive straight on, soon joining bridleway C58, then, at a sharp right-hand bend, turn left over a stile by a gate onto path GM18. Just past a pond, turn right over a stile and follow a right-hand hedge through two fields. At the far end of the second field, cross a stile and turn left onto path GM7a, following a left-hand hedge, with views over Ballinger Bottom to your right, to reach a stile into a wood. Cross this and follow a path straight on along the top edge of the wood. Where this path eventually bears right and descends, turn left through a squeeze-stile and follow a fenced path to a duck-under rail leading to a road in Ballinger.

Turn right onto this road and at a road junction, turn right again, then almost immediately turn left through a gate onto path GM7 and follow a grass path straight on through some allotments to a small gate into the end of a lane. Go through this gate, then turn right over a stile and turn left to follow a left-hand hedge to a stile into Hawthorn Wood. Cross this stile and follow waymarked path L29 straight on for some 300 yards, ignoring a crossing track with a gate to your left and passing a plantation. At the far end of the plantation turn right following the waymarked path to cross a stile into a field. Bear slightly right across the field to the end of a hedge ahead, then go past it and turn left following a left-hand hedge and later the garden fence of a much-extended cottage. Just past the cottage, join its drive and follow it straight on into a lane. At a junction of lanes by some cottages, turn left and follow a flinty lane (bridleway L42) uphill bearing right and then left to reach a gate and stile. Cross the stile and take path L42a following a right-hand hedge. Where the hedge turns right, leave it and take path GM3 straight on to a stile by a pylon where three hedges meet. Cross the stile and go diagonally across a field past another pylon to a stile. Having crossed this, go diagonally across another field to cross two further stiles, then continue straight on crossing a further field diagonally, passing the corner of a hedge to reach a gate by a tall oak left of a long cottage, which leads to the road at Potter Row.

Turn right onto this road, following it past several cottages, then, by the entrance to 'Silver Birches', turn left over a stile onto path GM2. Now follow a left-hand hedge to a gate and stile. Cross the stile and follow the left-hand hedge to a stile in it. Turn left over this and cross a narrow field, then turn right and follow a left-hand hedge to the far end of the field. Here go through a gap and bear slightly left across the next field, with a view of Great Missenden Church to your left, to two stiles. Cross these and continue straight on, joining a left-hand hedge by an ash tree and following it downhill to cross a stile in the bottom corner of the field. Now bear half left across a field to a stile, then cross three further fields diagonally, heading for a large green road sign on the A413. By this sign, cross two stiles to reach the A413, cross this road carefully and climb a stile by a gate. Now turn left onto path GM1e to a stile by a gate. Cross this stile and follow a right-hand hedge through two fields to a gate and kissing-gate leading to the A4128, then turn right for your starting point.

WALK 13: Great Kingshill

Length of Walk: 5.6 miles / 9.0 Km
Starting Point: Great Kingshill Sports Pavilion.
Grid Ref: SU878981
Maps: OS Landranger Sheet 165
OS Explorer Sheet 3
(or old Pathfinder Sheet 1138 SU89/99))
Chiltern Society FP Map No.12
How to get there/Parking: Great Kingshill, 3.2 miles
north of High Wycombe, may be reached from the town
centre by following the A4128 northwards towards Great
Missenden for 3.5 miles. In the village, by the 'Red Lion',
turn right and then right again into Common Road to the
car park on the edge of the village green.

Great Kingshill, the name of which derives from the manor
having been held by the Crown in Norman times, was, less
than 150 years ago, little more than a few scattered cottages
around a vast common. Following inclosure, however, when
the common was reduced to its present size, this hamlet
started to grow to become the relatively large village we know
today and it is for this reason that most of its buildings are of
Victorian or more modern origin. Like its neighbour
Prestwood, Great Kingshill was, at one time, noted for its
abundant cherry orchards, necessary for making the
Buckinghamshire speciality of cherry pie, but today most of
the orchards have unfortunately given way to the incessant
pressure for 'in-filling' development.

The walk soon leaves this outpost of suburbia behind and
explores the beautiful landscape of steep-sided ridges and
bottoms interspersed with Chiltern beechwoods to be found at
the head of the Hughenden Valley, before climbing to skirt
Prestwood on its way back to Great Kingshill.

Starting from Great Kingshill Sports Pavilion on the edge of the
green, take Common Road southwards for about 80 yards, then turn
right through a squeeze-stile onto path H58 and follow a left-hand
hedge across the recreation ground to a stile onto the A4128. Cross the
stile and the main road and take New Road straight on. At the far end

of New Road, turn left onto a fenced path (H60) and follow it to Pipers Lane. Turn right onto this road and follow it for quarter of a mile to the gates of Pipers Corner School. Here turn right over a stile by a gate onto path H54a, then turn immediately left and follow a left-hand tree-belt sheltering the school grounds with a fine view opening out to the right towards Naphill and Bryant's Bottom. Ignore a stile in the left-hand fence (where you join path H54 and the reverse direction of Walk 19), then, where the tree-belt bears left, go straight on across the field to a stile at the end of a hedge. Cross this stile and follow a fenced path along the edge of woodland to a stile in the right-hand fence. Turn right over this onto path H53 (leaving Walk 19) and go straight across the field, with a fine view ahead of the three 'bottoms' which converge to form the Hughenden Valley, aiming for the left-hand end of Hatches Wood to reach a stile. Cross this and continue straight on downhill to a stile into Hatches Lane. Turn left and follow this road downhill for quarter of a mile to a crossroads.

Here cross the major road and take path H1, the drive to Oakleaf Farm, straight on. On reaching the farm gate, keep left, taking a path between fences left of a bungalow straight on to a stile. Cross this and go straight on over a rise to a concealed stile, then bear half right across the corner of the next field to a gate and concealed stile (where you again meet but do not join the route of Walk 19). Here cross the stile and take path H49 straight on uphill, passing just right of a copse and a pair of Scots pine trees to reach a stile into Piggott's Wood. Inside the wood, disregard a path to the right. Now follow a waymarked path veering left and then right. After 100 yards, turn right at a waymarked junction onto path H47, then after a further 70 yards, turn left at another waymarked junction onto path H48 and follow this along the contours of the hill, ignoring all branching or crossing paths or tracks. After a third of a mile, disregard a path forking downhill to your right and go straight on until you reach a waymarked T-junction with path H42. Turn right onto this (joining Walk 15) and follow it downhill to reach a gate and stile out of the wood. Cross the stile and follow a left-hand hedge straight on to a stile and gate onto a road in Bryant's Bottom.

Having crossed this stile and road and a stile by a gate opposite, bear half right up a steep bank to a gate and stile by the corner of a garden hedge. Cross the stile and bear half right to a stile leading to a macadam drive. Cross the stile and turn right onto this drive (bridleway H37) leaving Walk 15 again. Now follow the drive through white gates, then swinging left then right around a large white house now known as 'Hughenden Chase'. Having passed the house, where a drive merges from the left, turn left over a stile onto the continuation of path H42, then turn right and follow a right-hand fence and tree-belt swinging right to reach another stile. Cross this and follow a right-hand hedge downhill to a stile onto a road near a road junction in Stony Green Bottom.

Turn left onto this road and follow it for a third of a mile passing a picnic site. On rounding a left-hand bend, pass a junction of right-hand hedges, then, some 40 yards further on, turn right through a kissing-gate by a gate onto path GM48 and bear half right across a field to enter Meadsgarden Wood in a corner. In the wood, go straight on uphill. Near the top of the hill, follow the path bearing right to reach a stile into a field. Cross this and follow the left-hand fence straight on across the field to a stile into Lawrence Grove Wood. Having crossed this, follow a woodland path straight on to reach a stile into another field. Now continue straight on, following a left-hand hedge across a dip to a gate and stile. Cross the stile and follow a path between hedges straight on to the A4128 on the edge of Prestwood.

Here turn right passing Prestwood's Victorian church. Opposite a flint cottage, turn left onto path GM48a, a rough track along the edge of a wood which narrows into a fenced path. At the far side of the right-hand field, turn right onto a crossing path into Peterley Wood, then immediately fork right onto bridleway GM43a. Now follow this obvious woodland bridleway straight on for over a third of a mile, ignoring all branching or crossing paths, until you reach a road. Cross this road and take path GM43 bearing slightly right to cross a stile into scrubland virtually opposite. At a fork just inside the scrubland, keep left and follow a winding path straight on for about 80 yards until you reach a crossing path (GM44). Turn right onto this and follow its winding course, disregarding crossing tracks and paths and soon entering and traversing a belt of mature woodland. At the far side of this woodland, take a fenced path straight on to reach a stile. Cross this and go past a pond, then bear half left across a field to a stile in the far corner. Having crossed this, follow a left-hand hedge, crossing another stile and taking enclosed path H79 joining a macadam drive and following it out to the A4128 on the edge of Great Kingshill. Turn left onto this road, then, at a road junction, turn left into Stag Lane and follow this road for some 250 yards. Now take the first turning right ('The Common') which leads you back to your point of departure.

WALK 13

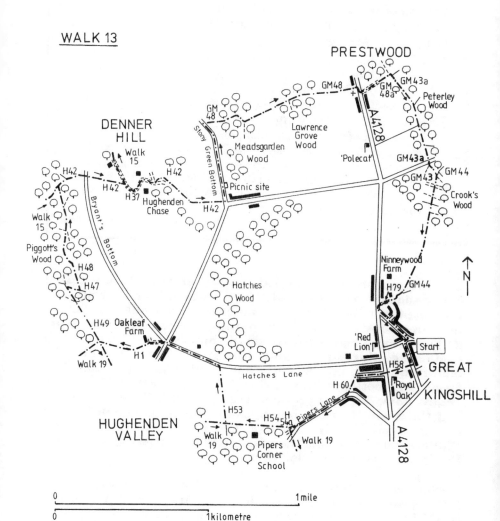

Length of Walk: 6.4 miles / 10.3 Km
Starting Point: 'Rising Sun', Little Hampden.
Grid Ref: SP858040
Maps: OS Landranger Sheet 165
OS Explorer Sheet 2
(or old Pathfinder Sheet 1118 (SP80/90))
Chiltern Society FP Maps Nos. 3 & 12
How to get there/Parking: Little Hampden, 2.6 miles
northwest of Great Missenden, may be reached from the
centre of the town by taking the Princes Risborough and
Ellesborough road westwards for two miles, then turning
right into a lane signposted to Little Hampden. A car park
is available on common land opposite the 'Rising Sun' at
the end of the road.

Little Hampden, on a high ridge at the end of a long winding
cul-de-sac lane, has often, with justification, been described as
the remotest village in the Buckinghamshire Chilterns. For all
this, an extensive network of inviting footpaths radiates from
it. This tiny village with its small thirteenth-century church
containing thirteenth- and fifteenth-century murals, its
picturesque old, but recently extended village pub and few
farms and cottages was, prior to 1885, a separate parish.
Today, however, it is grouped together with Great Hampden
and Hampden Row on the opposite side of Hampden Bottom
and it is principally this enlarged and particularly scenic
Chiltern parish which the walk explores, passing Hampden
House and Great Hampden Church.

Starting from the 'Rising Sun', take path G50, the right-hand of two
paths opposite the pub into woodland on Little Hampden Common.
Now follow this obvious waymarked path downhill. In the valley
bottom keep left, following the winding waymarked path to reach a
track at the edge of the wood. Do not join this track, but bear half left
through a hedge gap and follow the right-hand hedge downhill to a
corner of Hampdenleaf Wood. Here join a track entering the wood,
then immediately fork right. At a second fork, by the corner of a field

to your right, keep left following a waymarked track steeply uphill. Where this track forks again, bear right following a more gently climbing track to a path junction at the edge of a plantation. Here turn right onto G47 following a waymarked track along the edge of the plantation and then through a young plantation for over quarter of a mile until you reach a crossing path (G49). Turn left onto this path, soon crossing a stile to leave the wood. Now bear half right across a field to two stiles in the corner near two concealed bungalows. Cross these stiles and take a track (bridleway G46) straight on to reach Cobblershill Lane by Cobblershill Farm.

Turn right onto this road and follow it for quarter of a mile, disregarding a side-turning and a grassy track to the left. Just after a right-hand bend, turn left through a gate into a hedged grassy track (path G45). On emerging into a field, keep to this track, turning right and following a right-hand hedge to a gap in the corner of the field. Continue straight on through this and follow a defined path along the edge of a plantation, until you join a track and emerge into a field. Where the track turns right, leave it and follow the right-hand hedge straight on downhill to a hedge gap in the bottom corner of the field. Go through this and bear half left across the next field to a hedge gap at a road junction in Hampden Bottom.

Cross the major road and take Hotley Bottom Lane opposite, following this uphill for some 250 yards, then turn right onto path G44 up some steps and through a hedge gap into a fenced path. Now follow this uphill past a garden into a field, then follow the right-hand hedge straight on to a stile into Pepperboxes Wood. Inside the wood, follow a defined waymarked path straight on, ignoring a crossing track. Having passed through a plantation, turn left at a T-junction onto path G41, climbing between plantations to reach the edge of thinned mature woodland. Here turn right onto waymarked path G42 skirting the edge of the mature woodland at first, then bearing left into it. Now follow this path straight on through Lodge Wood, ignoring all crossing and branching paths until, after nearly half a mile, you reach a gate and stile leading onto Honor End Lane on the outskirts of Prestwood.

Turn left onto this road and, after about 150 yards, turn right into the drive to Nanfans Farm (path GM64). Where the drive turns right into the farm, leave it and go straight on over a stile by a gate. Now follow a right-hand fence to a stile into a field. Cross this stile and bear slightly right across the field to reach a stile in a dip. Having crossed this, go straight on uphill to join a left-hand fence and follow it to a further stile. Cross this, then bear slightly right across the field to the corner of a copse. Keeping left of the copse, follow its edge downhill. At its bottom corner, bear half right across the field to a flight of steps leading down to a road.

Turn right onto this road, then almost immediately left onto path G21 uphill through Rectory Wood, soon crossing a macadam drive. Continue straight on until the path merges with the drive which has looped to the left. Follow this drive straight on to a left-hand bend, then, where a gate comes into view in front of you, leave the track and go to the gate. Do not go through it, but instead turn left (now on bridleway G19) and follow a right-hand fence to the far end of the field. Here bear half left through a hedge gap and by a holly bush, turn right over a concealed stile onto path G22. Follow this fenced path through the trees and along the side of a field to a stile at the corner of the hedge. Cross this and continue straight on across a large field to a hedge gap right of an electricity pylon. Go through this, cross a road and go through a hedge gap opposite, then continue straight on across the next field to the corner of a hedge. Here follow a left-hand hedge straight on to a stile. Having crossed this, bear slightly right and follow an avenue of trees recently replenished by the planting of numerous saplings to a stile onto a road. Cross this road and go through a kissing-gate opposite (still on G22), then bear half right and follow the continuation of the avenue to another kissing-gate onto a macadam drive by Great Hampden Church.

Built in the thirteenth century Great Hampden Church contains various monuments to the Hampden family including its most famous member, John Hampden, cousin of Oliver Cromwell, whose refusal to pay King Charles I's unjust ship tax was one of the events leading to the Civil War. Wounded at the Battle of Chalgrove Field in 1643, John Hampden died soon after in Thame and was buried at Great Hampden, but his grave is unmarked. Nearby Hampden House, the seat of the Hampden family and their descendants, the Earls of Buckinghamshire till the Second World War, was partially built in the fourteenth century, considerably extended by John Hampden and much altered again in 1750.

Turn left onto the drive (bridleway G28) and follow it past the church and house to a set of gates. Go through these then turn right over a stile by gates onto path G34 and bear slightly left across a field to a stile into Lady Hampden's Wood. Cross this and follow a fenced path straight on through the wood, passing a large redwood tree on the left, to reach a gate and stile into a field. Here bear slightly left across the field to a stile by gates in the gap between two belts of trees in Hampden Bottom. Cross the stile and the road and go through gates opposite onto path E59. Now follow this track through a belt of trees called Coach Hedgerow uphill for a third of a mile until the track turns left into Widnell Wood. Turn right here and take path G64 straight across a field, heading towards the left-hand end of mature beechwood on the skyline, to reach a hedge gap. Go through this and

70

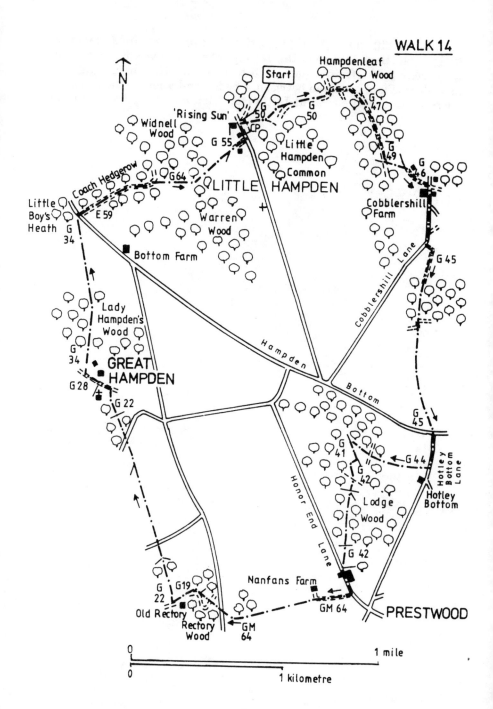

Start

Hampdenleaf Wood

'Rising Sun'

Widnell Wood

G 55

G 50

CP

G 50

G 47

G 49

G 6

Little Hampden Common

LITTLE HAMPDEN

Coach Hedgerow

G 64

Little Boy's Heath

E 59

G 34

Warren Wood

Cobblershill Farm

Cobblershill Lane

Bottom Farm

Lady Hampden's Wood

G 34

Hampden

Bottom

G 45

GREAT HAMPDEN

G 28

G 22

Honor End Lane

G 41

G 42

G 45

G 44

Hotley Bottom Lane

Hotley Bottom

Lodge Wood

G 42

G 22

G 19

Old Rectory

Rectory Wood

GM 64

Nanfans Farm

GM 64

PRESTWOOD

0   1 mile

0   1 kilometre

71

continue uphill through a plantation into another field. Here go straight on, then just past the far end of mature woodland to your right, bear half left onto path G55 to reach another hedge gap. Go through this and continue between a hedge and a fence, then along a concrete drive to the road at Little Hampden almost opposite the car park.

WALK 15:   Hampden Row

Length of Walk: 5.5 miles / 8.8 Km

Starting Point: 'Hampden Arms', Hampden Row.

Grid Ref: SP845015

Maps: OS Landranger Sheet 165
OS Explorer Sheets 2 (or old Pathfinder Sheet 1118 (SP80/90)) & 3 (or old Pathfinder Sheet 1138 (SU89/99)) Chiltern Society FP Map No.12

How to get there/Parking: Hampden Row, 5.4 miles northwest of High Wycombe, may be reached from the town by taking the A4128 northwards for two miles, leaving it at a roundabout where it turns right. Now go straight on up the Hughenden Valley for a further three-quarters of a mile. By the 'Harrow' turn right and after half a mile turn left following signposts to Bryant's Bottom. Follow this road through Bryant's Bottom for 2.3 miles to a crossroads. Turn right towards Hampden and Great Missenden and turn right again at a T-junction. At a road junction by the 'Hampden Arms', turn right and seek a parking place on the wide firm verges.

Hampden Row, the village attached to the Great Hampden estate, is typical of many such villages attached to major country estates in being some distance from its church and manor house on the edge of the parish common. Its name is, indeed, apt, as it consists largely of a pub and row of cottages along one side of a road with the common on the other which includes a particularly attractive cricket field laid out by the last Earl of Buckinghamshire in 1950. The village, or rather hamlet, derives its name from the Hampden family (later the Earls of Buckinghamshire) whose most famous member was John Hampden (1594 – 1643), the leading Parliamentarian politician and soldier.

The walk explores the heavily-wooded country of steep ridges and deep bottoms, so characteristic of Chiltern backland, visiting the village of Speen and the hamlets of Turnip End, Flowers Bottom, Upper North Dean and Denner Hill.

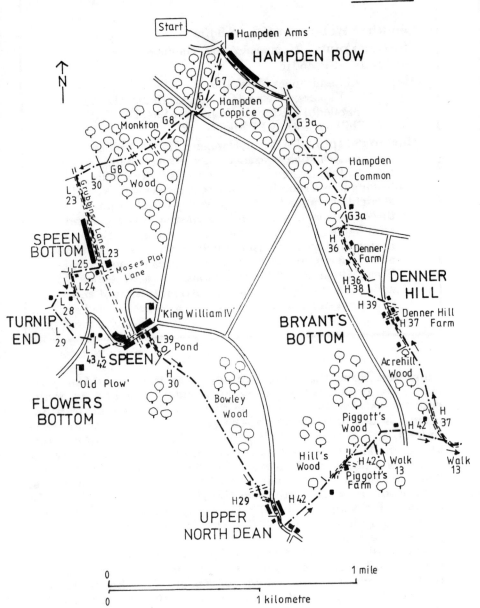

Starting from the 'Hampden Arms' at Hampden Row, take the Bryant's Bottom and High Wycombe road to the bus stop, then turn right onto path G7 along the edge of the cricket field. At the far side of the field, go straight on through a hedge gap to a stile into a wood called Hampden Coppice. Cross the stile and follow a path downhill near the right-hand edge of the wood, disregarding all branches to the left (later on path G6), to reach a road. Turn right onto this road and at a crossroads bear half left onto bridleway G8 through a fence gap into Monkton Wood. Just inside the wood, go through a squeeze-stile in the right-hand fence flanking this bridleway and follow a segregated footpath beside the fenced bridleway through the wood for nearly half a mile. Just before reaching a field ahead, go through a squeeze-stile to rejoin the bridleway. Now continue straight on, ignoring crossing paths and leaving Monkton Wood by a narrow hedged bridleway (L30). On reaching a rough road called Grubbins Lane (L23), turn left and follow it for a third of a mile. Opposite a corrugated iron barn, just before the junction with Moses Plat Lane, turn right onto path L25, at first between buildings and then between fences, and follow it downhill, soon entering an area of scrubland and descending some rough steps before dropping between a hedge and a fence to another rough road in Speen Bottom.

Turn left onto this road (L24) and after about 130 yards, by the gate to a mobile home, turn right onto a narrow path between a hedge and a fence (L28) to a set of rails. Cross these and follow a right-hand hedge uphill crossing another set of rails. Near the top, bear half left and continue to follow the hedge crossing a further set of rails then reaching a stile in the right-hand hedge leading to the hamlet of Turnip End. Do not cross this stile, but, instead, turn left onto path L29, crossing the field and descending to a stile near a large pylon in the hedge right of a farm in Flowers Bottom. Cross this and continue to a second stile onto a road. Cross this road and a stile opposite onto path L43, then take a fenced path crossing a stile and passing through a gate. Now take path L42 following a power-line straight on uphill to a stile then continue to a gate and stile onto a road at Speen.

Turn right onto this road and, just past a bus shelter, turn right again into Water Lane (L39). Where its macadam ends, cross a stile by a gate and follow a rough track straight on crossing a second stile by double gates and continuing to a third stile and gate by an attractive duck-pond. Cross the stile and take path H30 straight on disregarding a gate and stile to your left and following a left-hand fence for a third of a mile, ignoring a further stile in it and eventually reaching a stile and New Zealand (barbed-wire) gate. Cross this stile and continue straight on, gradually nearing Bowley Wood to your left. Having joined the edge of the wood, follow it, soon crossing a stile and following a left-hand hedge straight on downhill to a farm road. Cross the farm road and continue crossing a stile by a gate and following a left-hand hedge to cross a further stile. Now take path H29 straight on soon with a farm building to your right, to a stile and gate leading into a lane which brings you out onto a road at Upper North Dean.

Turn right onto this road and soon after the end of the houses on the right, turn left onto H42, a fenced path leading to a stile. Cross this stile and follow a left-hand hedge uphill to a stile into the corner of Hill's Wood. Cross the stile and follow a path along the inside edge of the wood, continuing uphill and ignoring all branching paths to the left, until the path leaves the wood and joins a macadam drive. Follow this drive (still H42) straight on past Piggott's Farm, disregarding a branching drive to the right. By a galvanised left-hand gate just before Piggott's Wood, fork slightly right off the drive into the wood. Where the path forks, bear right and follow a well-defined path, ignoring all branching and crossing paths, downhill through the wood joining Walk 13 and eventually reaching a stile. Cross this and follow a left-hand hedge straight on downhill to a stile and gate onto a road in Bryant's Bottom. Having crossed this stile and road and a stile by a gate opposite, bear half right up a steep bank to a gate and stile by the corner of a garden hedge. Cross the stile and bear half right to a stile leading to a macadam drive. Cross the stile and turn left onto this drive (bridleway H37) leaving Walk 13 again. Now follow the drive to its end near Denner Hill House, then go straight on through white gates into a narrow bridleway which later widens into a track. Follow this straight on for half a mile past Denner Hill Farm to the end of a macadam road at the hamlet of Denner Hill.

Here, opposite a right-hand cottage, turn left through a kissing-gate by a gate onto path H39 and bear half right across a field to a stile in a hedge gap. Cross this stile and turn right onto path H38, following a right-hand hedge to a gate and rails. Having crossed the rails, bear slightly left across the next field (now on path H36) to a gate and stile left of farm buildings at Denner Farm. Cross the stile and follow a drive past the farm, turning right where the drive does to reach a gate. Go through this gate and turn left over a stile by gates onto path G3a into scrubland on Hampden Common. Now follow a waymarked path across this confusing common. At a waymarked fork, take the left-hand option straight on, then at a crossways, ignore a crossing path and bear slightly left. Soon after this, in a clearing on a slight rise, take the right-hand fork and continue straight on to a further clearing. Go straight on to the far end of this clearing where you reach a stony track leading to gates and a stile then continuing along a macadam drive to a road. Turn right onto this, bear left at a double junction and follow the road for a third of a mile back to the 'Hampden Arms'.

WALK 16:   Whiteleaf Hill

Length of Walk: 6 miles / 9.6 Km

Starting Point: Whiteleaf Hill car park.

Grid Ref: SP824035

Maps: OS Landranger Sheet 165
   OS Explorer Sheet 2
   (or old Pathfinder Sheet 1118 (SP80/90))
   Chiltern Society FP Map No.3.

How to get there/Parking: Whiteleaf Hill car park, one mile east of Princes Risborough may be reached from the town by taking the A4010 towards Aylesbury to Monks Risborough and turning right onto a road signposted to Whiteleaf and Hampden. Follow this straight on up Whiteleaf Hill to a left-hand car park near the hilltop.

Whiteleaf Hill, a wooded hill on the Chiltern escarpment above Princes Risborough, is noteworthy for the large chalk cross cut in the turf on the hillside. Although there is some doubt as to its antiquity, the consensus of expert opinion is that it is of Saxon or even Ancient British origin. On a clear day, the cross is visible for at least 20 miles.

The walk takes you through the heavily wooded escarpment backland to Buckmoorend near Chequers, the Prime Minister's country retreat in the upper part of Hampden Bottom. It then returns by way of the escarpment using parts of the Ridgeway Path taking in Pulpit Hill, the secluded leafy hamlet of Lower Cadsden and the summit of Whiteleaf Hill with its fine views across the Vale of Aylesbury, where Whiteleaf Cross can be seen from above.

Starting from the vehicular entrance to Whiteleaf Hill car park, head westwards through the car park then take a hoggined path straight on across a mown grass picnic area to reach the Ridgeway Path (R13) in the trees ahead. Turn right onto this and by the far end of the right-hand field, turn right onto signposted bridleway R21a passing through a fence gap and continuing along the inside edge of the wood for a third of a mile. Where the bridleway forks and the right-hand

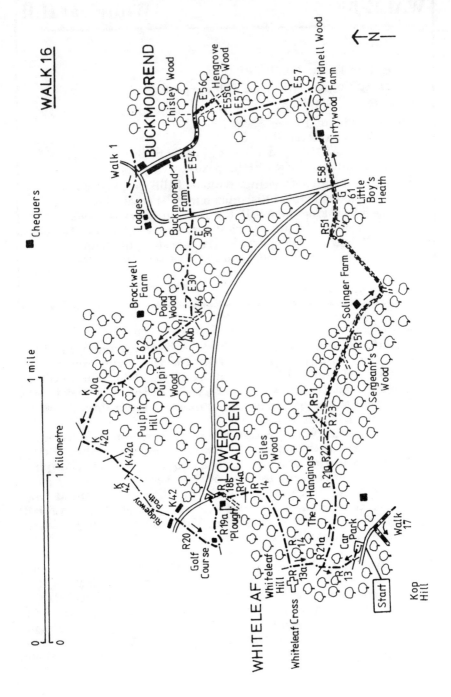

option begins a gradual climb, go left through a squeeze-stile onto path R22 descending slowly. Where a wooden fence blocks your way ahead, bear right and at a T-junction turn left onto bridleway R23, following it downhill and ignoring a crossing track. At a multiple path junction by a gate, turn right onto path R51, crossing a stile and soon merging with an old track from the right. Follow this track straight on through Sergeant's Wood for a third of a mile until you emerge from the wood by double gates at Solinger Farm.

Here turn right onto a macadam drive (still R51) and follow it downhill. In the valley bottom continue to follow the drive which bears left and loses its macadam surface. After a further quarter of a mile it bears right, passes through a copse called Little Boy's Heath (now as G61) and reaches a road in Hampden Bottom. Cross the road bearing slightly right and take path E58, a rough track virtually opposite, to Dirtywood Farm. On reaching the farm, bear left then right passing left of the farm, then follow a right-hand hedge uphill to a gap which leads you into a corner of Widnell Wood. Inside the wood, follow the waymarked path uphill, ignoring a branching path to the right, then, at a fork, bear right. On reaching a waymarked junction near the top of the hill, turn sharp left and follow a waymarked woodland path (E57) for a third of a mile until you reach a crossing path along the inside edge of Hengrove Wood. Turn right onto this path (E55a) climbing slowly. Just beyond a squeeze-stile, at a fork continue straight on uphill until you reach a crossing track. Turn left onto this track (path E56) and follow it to a stile by gates onto a narrow road. Turn left onto the road and follow it for some 300 yards to the edge of Buckmoorend.

Just before the first left-hand cottage, turn left through a hedge gap onto path E54 and follow a right-hand garden fence past the garden. Where the fence turns right, bear slightly right across the field to a gap roughly in the middle of the belt of trees ahead. Go through this gap and out to a road. Turn left onto the road then almost immediately right onto a rough track (bridleway E30) which leads you into a field. Do not enter this field, but bear slightly right along a fenced bridleway which leads you into a finger of Pond Wood. Now follow an obvious bridleway through the wood. After quarter of a mile, on reaching a plantation, follow the waymarked path, bearing left, ignoring a right-hand fork, then later bearing right (now on K46) and reaching a crossing bridleway (K40b). Turn right onto this and follow it (later E62) straight on for three-quarters of a mile ignoring all branching tracks and paths. After more than half a mile, near the top of Pulpit Hill (formerly known as 'Bullpit Hill'), your track (now K40a) leaves Pulpit Wood and briefly permits you a fine view of the Vale of Aylesbury before you start to descend in a gully through scrubland.

A few yards past a right-hand kissing-gate where you join the Ridgeway Path, turn left onto K42a, a narrow path over the bank of the gully, then descend steeply to a kissing-gate. Go through the kissing-gate and continue straight on across a dip. On the far side of the dip, join the edge of a left-hand belt of thick scrub concealing an old fenceline and follow it straight on for some 250 yards, ignoring a crossing path and reaching a kissing-gate into a slightly sunken crossing bridleway (K41). Here bear half-right crossing the bridleway and continuing to follow the Ridgeway Path (now on path K42) passing through a belt of scrub and taking a crop-break straight on across a field to a kissing-gate left of a group of pines ahead. Go through the kissing-gate into a fenced path and follow this steeply downhill to a kissing-gate onto a road. Cross the road and a stile by a gate opposite onto path R20 which leads you onto a golf course. (Beware of driving golfers!) Now follow a left-hand hedge uphill along the edge of the golf course. At the far end of the hedge, turn left over a stile and follow an enclosed path (R19a) to Lower Cadsden.

Here turn right onto the side-road and follow it past the 'Plough', originally opened for the local chair bodgers working in the woods, to the entrance to the pub car park. Turn right here, following the Ridgeway Path (R18b) uphill through Giles Wood. After some 70 yards, go left at a fork, go through a kissing-gate by a gate and follow path R14a (later R14) bearing right at a fork and ignoring a crossing path and climbing through the woods for nearly half a mile until you emerge by a kissing-gate into the hilltop clearing directly above Whiteleaf Cross. Now turn left and follow the somewhat worn Ridgeway Path (R13a/R13) through woodland along the ridgetop for quarter of a mile to Whiteleaf Hill car park.

WALK 17:   Princes Risborough

Length of Walk: 6.1 miles / 9.9 Km
Starting Point: Market Hall, Princes Risborough.
Grid Ref: SP807035
Maps: OS Landranger Sheet 165
OS Explorer Sheet 2
(or old Pathfinder Sheet 1118 (SP80/90))
Chiltern Society FP Maps Nos. 3 & 7
Parking: Princes Risborough offers adequate facilities for
on- or off-street parking including a car park west of the
church.

Princes Risborough, in the Risborough Gap in the Chiltern
escarpment, derives the first part of its name from the Black
Prince who reputedly built a castle or palace here. For many
centuries, Princes Risborough was a small market town and
this has left its mark in the wealth of attractive cottages,
houses and shops around the market hall which itself dates
from 1824. The church dates mainly from the thirteenth
century, but the tower had to be rebuilt in 1804 following the
collapse of its predecessor and only gained its spire in 1907.
Within the last fifty years, however, the town has become
swamped with insensitive modern development leaving its
centre as a pleasant oasis in the middle of a suburban desert.

The walk leaves the town behind after half a mile and leads
you over rolling open foothills with fine views across the
Risborough Gap and up to Lacey Green with its windmill. It
then takes you for some distance along the upland plateau
with open fields at first and a wealth of peaceful woodland
later before descending Kop Hill with its extensive views back
into Princes Risborough.

Starting from the market hall in the centre of Princes Risborough,
follow the High Street southeastwards. At a T-junction with the
A4010, turn right onto it and after about 200 yards, just past a filling
station, turn left onto a macadam path (R3b) roughly opposite Park
Street. Follow this straight on uphill for some 170 yards to a set of

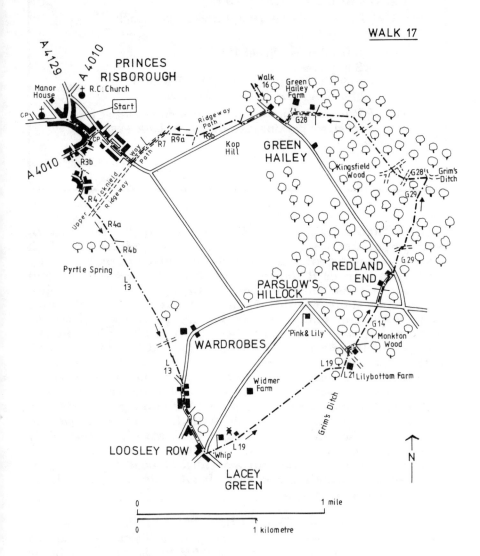

safety barriers then turn right onto a branching path which leads you out to a bend in a road. Turn left onto this road and follow it straight on to its end. Here go straight on through a hedge gap into a field, then turn left onto path R4, following the left-hand hedge, with fine views of the Vale of Aylesbury over your right shoulder, to reach a hedge gap in the corner of the field which leads you onto the Upper Icknield Way. Cross this Ancient British road, now a rough lane, and cross a stile opposite. Now follow path R4a straight on downhill with a fence to your right to the left-hand end of a line of trees shading Pyrtle Spring. Here take path R4b straight on past the spring and follow a right-hand fence uphill to a stile. Cross this and take path L13 straight on over a hill, heading towards the right-hand end of a group of trees to the right of the hamlet of Wardrobes. In the next dip, cross a stile and go straight on across a field climbing to the corner of a hedge, then follow the hedge straight on to a stile. Cross the stile, a macadam drive and another stile opposite and follow a left-hand hedge straight on to another corner of the field. Here turn left over a stile, then bear right across a field to another stile. Cross this and bear half left to a hedge gap in the far corner of the field which leads you out to a road junction.

Here join the major road and follow it straight on uphill for nearly half a mile ignoring a side road to the right. On reaching Lacey Green at the top of the hill, just past the crossroads by the 'Whip' turn left over a stile by a bus shelter onto path L19 and follow a left-hand hedge. The windmill to your left, the oldest surviving smock mill in the country, was originally built at Chesham in the late seventeenth century, but was dismantled and rebuilt on its present site in 1821. After becoming disused in 1920, the mill became very dilapidated, but was painstakingly restored in the 1970s by Chiltern Society volunteers. Now cross a stile and continue to follow the left-hand hedge, crossing another stile and where the hedge turns away to the left, go straight on across a field to a stile. Having crossed this, continue straight on across a paddock, then cross a stile and bear slightly right to a further stile. Cross this and follow a right-hand fence crossing three further stiles and continuing to a stile by a gate. Now follow a left-hand fence, then, where a hedge begins, continue straight on across the field to a stile. Cross this and bear half right across a field to a stile which leads you into a tree-lined bridleway on the line of the ancient earthwork known as Grim's Ditch. Turn left onto this bridleway (L21) and follow it out to a road at Lilybottom Farm.

Turn left onto the road and at the far end of a right-hand cottage garden, turn right onto bridleway G14 towards Monkton Wood. Just past the back of the garden, keep left at two forks and enter a plantation. Follow the obvious bridleway straight on for quarter of a mile until you emerge by way of a bridlegate and stile at a road junction. Here cross the major road and continue straight on along a road through the tiny woodland hamlet of Redland End to another road junction. Turn left onto the major road and, after a few yards, turn right over a stile onto path G29 into Kingsfield Wood. Follow this obvious path straight on along the line of an ancient earthwork (still Grim's Ditch). Where a track crosses the earthwork, bear slightly right and follow the waymarks to a fork. Here go left and follow an obvious path roughly parallel to Grim's Ditch for some 250 yards to a stile which leads you out of the wood. Follow the outside edge of the wood straight on, later with a plantation to your right, until you reach a crossing track.

Here turn left onto a waymarked segregated footpath on the near side of bridleway G28 and follow it for nearly quarter of a mile, ignoring a major crossing track, to reach a waymarked junction. Ignore a crossing track and take a fenced bridleway straight on downhill. At the bottom of the dip, go through a squeeze-stile in the left-hand fence and follow a segregated footpath alongside the fence until you reach the edge of the wood. Here go through a gap in the wire to rejoin the fenced bridleway and follow it uphill, later widening into a farm road. Now follow this farm road straight on becoming macadamed and reaching a gate and stile by Green Hailey Farm. Cross the stile, then turn left onto a macadam farm drive and follow it out to a road. Turn right onto the road and, at a road junction, turn left. After some 250 yards, where the road starts to descend Kop Hill, turn right over a stile onto the Ridgeway Path (R9b). At first keep close to the road passing left of a large clump of bushes, then continue straight on to a kissing-gate concealed by another clump of bushes. Go through this and continue straight on downhill through scrubland. Disregard a crossing path and (now on path R9a) soon emerge from the scrub by a stile. Follow a left-hand fence straight on through two fields to a hedge gap onto the Upper Icknield Way (R7). Turn left into this lane and follow it for nearly quarter of a mile to a road. Turn right onto this and follow it for quarter of a mile to a roundabout. Here turn left, then turn right for the market hall.

WALK 18: Smalldean Bottom (Nr.Bradenham)

Length of Walk: (A) :   5.5 miles / 8.8 Km
                       (B) :   2.5 miles / 4.0 Km
                       (C) :   3.4 miles / 5.4 Km

Starting Point: (A/B/C) National Trust car park, Smalldean Bottom.

Grid Ref: SU823990

Maps: OS Landranger Sheet 165
        OS Explorer Sheets 2 (or old Pathfinder Sheet 1118 (SP80/90)) (A/B only) & 3 (or old Pathfinder Sheet 1138 (SU89/99)) (all)
        Chiltern Society FP Map No.7

How to get there/Parking: The car park in Smalldean Bottom, 4.5 miles northwest of High Wycombe, may be reached from the town by taking the A40 westwards to the Pedestal at West Wycombe and forking right here onto the A4010. Follow this for 2.5 miles to the 'Golden Cross' crossroads, then turn right into a lane signposted Smalldean Lane and follow it for three-quarters of a mile to an unsignposted right-hand car park about 200 yards beyond Smalldean Farm.

Smalldean Bottom, a peaceful combe leading off the Saunderton valley into the hills, is followed by a narrow winding lane, at one point straddled by a farm. The National Trust, which owns the sizeable Bradenham Estate, has provided a car park here for walkers from which all the alternative walks start.

All three walks include some fine views across the wide Saunderton valley with alternatives A & B passing through open hill country and visiting the twin villages of Lacey Green and Loosley Row and alternatives A & C visiting the picturesque village of Bradenham, one-time home of Disraeli, and returning through pleasant beechwoods.

Starting from the National Trust car park in Smalldean Bottom, Walk C turns left along Smalldean Lane and follows it to a right-hand cottage at Smalldean Farm. Now omit the next three paragraphs.

Walks A and B, however, turn right along Smalldean Lane and after about 200 yards, turn left through a kissing-gate by a white gate.

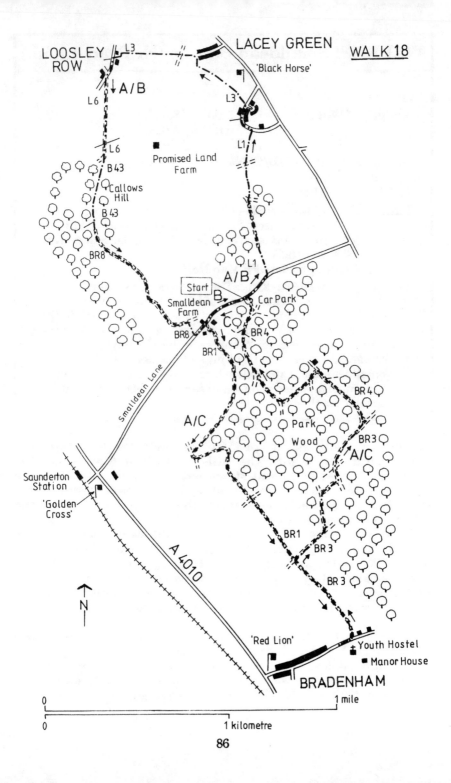

Now follow path L1 beside a right-hand hedge to two gates and a kissing-gate. Go through the kissing-gate and follow a fenced track straight on. By a right-hand copse, disregard a track to your right and a gate to your left and follow a fenced path straight on to a small gate. Go through this gate, cross a farm track and another stile and continue straight on along another fenced path to a road at Lacey Green.

Turn left here and follow the road, bending gradually to the right and passing some old cottages. Ignore one footpath to the left, then, opposite Hambye Close, turn left over a stile by a gate onto path L3 and bear half right across a field to a stile. Cross this stile and bear half left across the corner of the next field to another stile, after crossing which a fine view is obtained across the Saunderton valley. Bear half right across the corner of the field to a stile. Cross this and continue straight on across the next field to a stile in the far corner which leads you into a path between hedges which emerges at the end of a residential road. Turn left here (still on L3) into a gully path downhill to a farm road. Cross this and go straight on uphill between hedges to cross a stile at the top. Now continue downhill between a hedge and a fence. Eventually the path turns left then right around a garden fence before emerging at a road in the hillside village of Loosley Row.

Turn left along the road and, at a road junction, turn left over a stile by a gate. In so doing, do not fail to look at the embossed metal stile steps, produced by the two hundred year old village forge, giving information about the locality. Now take path L6 following a track beside a left-hand fence with extensive views opening out behind you. At the far end of the field, cross a stile into a belt of woodland and follow the obvious path B43 straight on through it for quarter of a mile. On reaching a gate and stile, cross the stile, leave the wood and take path BR8 following a left-hand hedge downhill through three fields until you reach the corner of an orchard at Smalldean Farm. Here turn right crossing a stile and emerging into Smalldean Lane, then turn left and follow this road for about 100 yards to a left-hand cottage.

Here **Walk B** continues straight on along the lane to reach the car park. **Walks A and C** go through the right-hand of two farm gates opposite the cottage onto path BR1, then beyond the farm buildings take a grassy track bearing half left and soon following a left-hand fence. On reaching Park Wood, ignore a kissing-gate in its fence and continue straight on along its outside edge. After a further third of a mile, the track reaches a hedge gap at the end of a protruding finger of woodland. Here turn left and at another hedge gap, turn left again (still on BR1) and follow the edge of the wood steeply uphill through a kissing-gate by a field-gate. Near the top of the hill, ignore a kissing-gate into the wood and turn right following the outside edge of the wood along the contours. By this point, a fine view has opened out down the valley towards High Wycombe and, on rounding a bend, Bradenham with its manor house and church comes into view. The manor house, originally built in the mid-sixteenth century, but much altered in the seventeenth and early nineteenth centuries, is principally known today as the one-time home of the writer Isaac Disraeli and his son, Benjamin, later to become Prime Minister. The church, built in about 1100, boasts two of the oldest bells in the country, dating from about 1300, and a plaque to the Christian convert, Isaac Disraeli, while the village around its attractive green has been spared from modern expansion thanks to being owned and preserved by the National Trust.

On passing through more gates, ignore a crossing track entering Park Wood and soon leave the edge of the wood behind. Disregard a second crossing track and continue straight on along path BR3 to two stiles and gates leading past the youth hostel into Bradenham village. After exploring this attractive little village, retrace your steps along path BR3 past the youth hostel, over the two stiles and along the track until you reach a crossing track. Now turn right and follow this fenced track (still BR3) up the combe until you enter Park Wood. Here turn left onto a wide fire-break climbing to reach a clearing at its far end, where there is a fine view of Bradenham Church and Manor House behind you. At the clearing turn right onto a track downhill and at the bottom, turn left onto a wide track. This track bears first right and then left, becoming path BR4 and climbing to reach a right-hand building. Just before this building, turn left onto a bridle track, then, near the top of the rise, fork right onto a waymarked path. Disregard a major curving track to your right and a crossing track, then turn left onto a waymarked path and follow it for nearly half a mile ignoring all branching paths until you emerge from Park Wood at the car park.

WALK 19:	Hughenden

Length of Walk: 6.3 miles / 10.1 Km

Starting Point: Hughenden Church car park.

Grid Ref: SU865955

Maps: OS Landranger Sheet 165
OS Explorer Sheet 3 (or old Pathfinder Sheet
1138 (SU89/99))
Chiltern Society FP Map No.12

How to get there/Parking: Hughenden Church, 1.5 miles
north of High Wycombe, may be reached from the town by
following the A4128 northwards for 1.5 miles and turning
left onto a side-road signposted to Hughenden Manor.
Cross a cattle grid, then take a left fork to a parking area
in front of the church.

Notes: Heavy nettle growth may be encountered on path
H56 in summer.

Hughenden, formerly 'Hitchenden', is a name given to a
parish, its church and its manor house, but no ancient village
of this name exists. The church and nearby manor house both
have close links with the Victorian prime minister, Benjamin
Disraeli, who owned Hughenden Manor from 1848 until his
death in 1881. He entertained Queen Victoria there in 1877 and
during his time there extensively remodelled the
eighteenth-century house, the park and the thirteenth-century
church according to his own eccentric taste. He is buried in
the churchyard and a plaque in his memory was erected near
his accustomed pew by Queen Victoria in 1882.

The walk explores some of the ridges and deep valleys on
either side of the Hughenden valley, visiting the extensive
commons of Downley and Naphill and the hilltop villages of
Naphill and Cryers Hill, as well as combining a fair mixture of
woodland and open country with fine views.

Starting from the parking area, go back to the fork in the road and
turn left onto the other road, soon passing the church to the left and
reaching a cattle grid and bridlegate. Go through the gate and follow
the road to its end, passing Hughenden Manor to the left. At the end
of the road, take a rough bridleway (H15) straight on, dropping

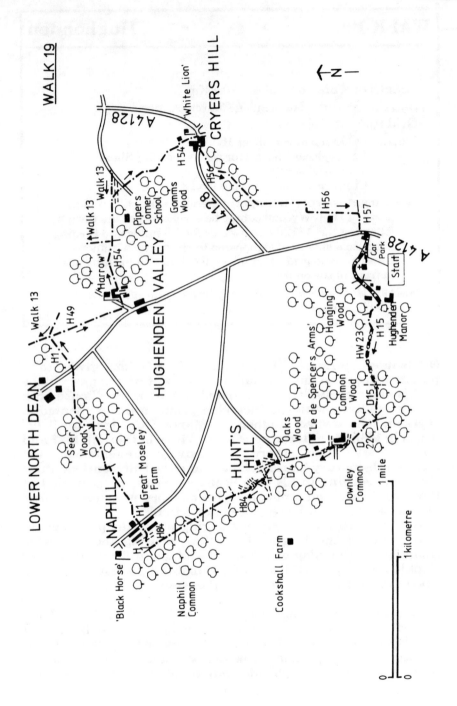

WALK 19

LOWER NORTH DEAN

CRYERS HILL

'White Lion'

A4128

A4128

A4128

Walk 13

Walk 13

Walk 13

Pipers Corner School

Gomms Wood

H54

H56

H56

H56

H57

'Harrow'

H54

H49

H1

Start

Car Park

Seer Wood

Walk 13

Hanging Wood

'Le de Spencers Arms'

HW 23

H15

Hughenden Manor

HUGHENDEN VALLEY

NAPHILL

Great Moseley Farm

H1

Common Wood

D15

'Black Horse'

H1

H84

HUNT'S HILL

Oaks Wood

D4

D 22

Downley Common

Naphill Common

H84

Cookshall Farm

N

1 mile

1 kilometre

0

0

90

through Hanging Wood and bearing right. At a fork, bear left and continue downhill through the wood, ignoring a crossing path and emerging onto a fenced track along a valley bottom (now on bridleway HW23). After quarter of a mile, this enters Common Wood. Here take bridleway D15 straight on along the valley bottom for about 300 yards, disregarding all branching tracks, then, by a large right-hand oak tree with a yellow 'H' painted on it to mark a hydrant, turn right onto bridleway D22. Now follow this uphill, bearing left at a fork and soon emerging onto Downley Common.

Continue straight on, joining a rough track (path D4) at a bend in it. Follow this straight on past the end of a macadam road and the 'Le de Spencers Arms' (the former title of the Dashwoods of West Wycombe). At the end of the right-hand row of cottages, take a wide path straight on between posts into Oaks Wood and, not deviating to right or left, continue past several pits to another set of posts leading out to the end of a macadam road. Here take a rough road straight on, bearing left at a fork. Where the gardens to your right end, follow the main track bearing left. After passing under a power line, turn right onto a track (bridleway H84).

Naphill Common, on which you now are, is noted for its oaks, believed to have been the original Chiltern tree species. Just past a large pond bear right then immediately fork left and at a T-junction turn left again. Now (still on bridleway H84) go straight on for over half a mile ignoring all crossing or branching tracks and paths, soon passing a large clearing to your right and then continuing along a wide woodland track until you pass through a small clearing ringed with small yew trees. Here, at a waymarked crossways with a close pair of oaks surrounded by holly to your left, turn right onto path H1, soon emerging from Naphill Common opposite No.1, Dene Cottages. Cross a rough track here and take a hedged path right of this cottage through to the main road at Naphill.

Cross this and a stile opposite and pass through a squeeze-stile then follow a left-hand hedge to a holly tree. Here bear slightly right across the field to a gate and stile in the far corner. Having crossed the stile, go straight on across a field, keeping right of some bushes and two small trees, to reach a hedge gap. Now follow a left-hand hedge straight on through a further field to a corner of Seer Wood. Here bear half left into the wood then bear slightly right onto an obvious path downhill into a valley bottom. Just past a large clump of holly bushes, bear half left and follow a winding path to a stile at the edge of the wood. Cross this and bear half right across a field to another stile. Having crossed this, bear half left across the next field to a stile near the right-hand end of a line of trees at the North Dean road. Cross this stile and the road then go through double gates opposite and follow a left-hand hedge uphill to a stile and gate in it near the top of the rise, where you briefly meet the route of Walk 13. Here turn right onto path H49, descending the field to a kissing-gate in a hedge ga p opposite the 'Harrow' in Hughenden Valley.

Cross the road and take path H54 right of the 'Harrow' through its car park to a stile. Having crossed this, follow a fenced path uphill, crossing the end of a road, climbing a flight of steps and entering a wood. Follow the fenced path steeply uphill through the wood. On emerging at the top, follow a left-hand fence straight on past an ash thicket until the path again becomes enclosed between fences. Disregard the stile of a crossing path and continue straight on (rejoining the reverse direction of Walk 13), until you cross a stile into a field. Now go straight on across the field, joining a right-hand hedge and following it to a stile in it. Turn right over this stile (parting company with Walk 13) and bear half left across the drive to Pipers Corner School. Now follow a right-hand hedge to a stile onto a road called Boss Lane. Cross this stile and the road and go through a kissing-gate opposite. Now, still on H54, follow the right-hand side of a fence straight on to a stile. Having crossed this, take a fenced path past Gomms Wood to a hedge gap, then follow a left-hand hedge to a gap at the corner of a school fence. Go through this and follow a path between the fence and a hedge to the A4128 at Cryers Hill.

Turn right along this road and after the last left-hand house, cross the road and take path H56 through a former gateway. Now follow a left-hand hedge and line of trees through several fields, then enter a belt of trees by a kissing-gate. Here follow an obvious path which later leaves the trees behind, turns left and passes between hedges for quarter of a mile, until you emerge over a stile into a field. Turn right here and follow a right-hand hedge to the corner of the field, then turn left and follow the right-hand hedge past a barn to a stile at the far end of the field. Cross this and drop down into sunken bridleway H57, then turn right and follow it downhill to the A4128. Turn left along this road and after about 70 yards, turn right into the road to Hughenden Church and Manor.

WALK 20:   High Wycombe (The Rye)

Length of Walk: 7.0 miles / 11.3 Km or 8.6 miles / 13.8 Km
Starting Point: Wycombe District Council noticeboard in
   rear corner of the swimming pool car park on The Rye.
Grid Ref: SU874923
Maps: OS Landranger Sheet 175
         OS Explorer Sheet 3 (or old Pathfinder Sheets 1138
         (SU89/99) & 1157 (SU88/98))
         Chiltern Society FP Maps Nos. 1 & 13
How to get there/Parking: From High Wycombe town
   centre, take the A40 towards London for three-quarters of
   a mile. Just after the 'Pheasant' roundabout, turn right
   into Bassetsbury Lane and after 300 yards turn right
   again to reach the swimming pool car park. Should the car
   park be full or closed, on-street parking is possible in
   nearby side-streets.

High Wycombe, formerly known as Chepping Wycombe, is
today a sprawling modern industrial town, but was once an
exceptionally attractive rural market town as its old name
suggests. A number of the buildings which contributed to its
former beauty remain such as its thirteenth-century church
with later additions, the Guildhall dominating the High Street
built by the Earl of Shelburne in 1757 and the octagonal
Market Hall built in 1604 and remodelled in 1761, but many of
the others have been demolished or disfigured by modern
shop fronts. Despite all this modern development, however, a
'green lung' has been preserved reaching into the town centre
in the form of the town's ancient common, The Rye, and the
adjacent parks of Wycombe Abbey and Daws Hill House.
   The walk, though starting on The Rye less than
three-quarters of a mile from the town centre, is one of
surprising beauty exploring an 'island' of rural tranquillity
surrounded by conurbations and major roads. Having soon left
the town behind, it leads you over the high ridge separating
the Wye and Thames valleys, where extensive beechwoods
alternate with fine open views, to the picturesque village of
Little Marlow, where a detour to the banks of the Thames is
possible, the return being by a similar parallel route.

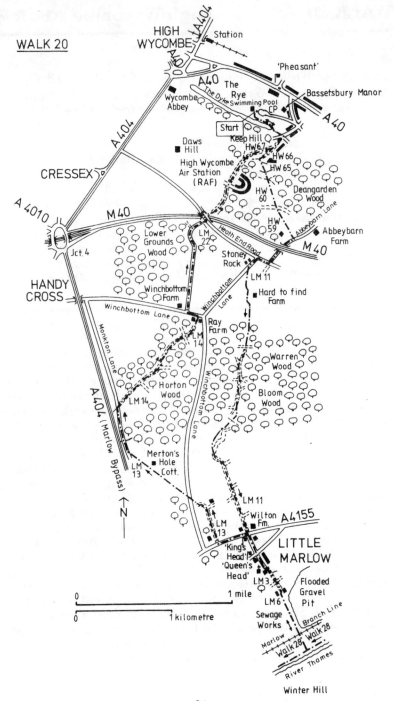

WALK 20

94

Starting from the District Council noticeboard in the far corner of the swimming pool car park on The Rye where the site of a Roman villa was excavated in 1954, take a macadam path to reach the bank of the ornamental lake known as The Dyke. This lake was constructed in the late eighteenth century by the Earl of Shelburne on the line of the old Windsor road as part of the park of Wycombe Abbey. Here turn left along its edge and at the end of the lake, take a terraced path above the river straight on, keeping right at a fork, to reach Warrenwood Drive. Now cross the road and take a macadam track opposite uphill. Where the macadam surface ends, fork left onto path HW66, a grassy track along the back of gardens. At the end of the houses, turn left still following a garden hedge. On reaching a fork, bear right onto path HW65 climbing steeply into Deangarden Wood. Soon ignore a crossing path and take path HW60 straight on uphill to a stile leading out of the wood. Cross this stile and bear half left following the outside edge of the wood and soon passing through an outcrop of scrub. On reaching a grassy track by a corner of the wood, take path HW59 straight on through a kissing-gate and across a field to a second kissing-gate. Now go straight on heading for an electricity pylon to the left of a tall radio mast to reach a stile leading to Abbeybarn Lane.

Turn right onto this road, soon passing under the M40 and reaching a T-junction at Stoney Rock. Here turn right into Heath End Road, then after 150 yards turn left into Winchbottom Lane. After about 100 yards, by the second right-hand cottage, turn left through a kissing-gate onto path LM11 and follow a left-hand hedge with fine views ahead down Winchbottom towards Ashley Hill and to your right across this bottom towards Handy Cross. At the far end of the field, by Hard-to-find Farm, turn left over a stile and follow the left-hand fence to the field corner. here turn right and follow the left-hand hedge to a stile into Warren Wood.

Now follow a woodland path straight on until you reach a crossing track at the edge of an open area. Cross this track and take a path straight on into regenerating woodland, soon joining a track, then at a fork, bear right shortly re-entering mature beechwoods. Here ignore a crossing track and continue straight on for a further 300 yards descending gradually. Where the major track begins to swing to the right, leave it and take a waymarked path (still LM11) straight on soon reaching a field. Here follow the left-hand hedge straight on to a stile in it, then cross this with a panoramic view opening out with Bourne End backed by Cliveden Woods to your left, Little Marlow and Winter Hill ahead and Marlow backed by Ashley Hill to your right. Now turn right into a sunken way beside a right-hand hedge following it downhill, later joining a farm track and continuing along it for a further half a mile to the A4155 at Little Marlow opposite the 'Kings Head'.

If wishing to explore this attractive village or make a detour to the River Thames, take the village street straight on into Little Marlow. Of particular interest are the sixteenth-century Manor House, which has been much extended and altered over the centuries, and the twelfth-century church of St. John the Baptist with its fourteenth-century tower where the well-known thriller writer, Edgar Wallace (1875 – 1932), is buried, but there are also a number of typical Chiltern sixteenth- to eighteenth-century cottages which complete the idyllic village setting. If wishing to go to the river, continue to the end of the village street, then take path LM3, a private road, straight on, later narrowing to footpath LM6 and crossing the Marlow Branch railway to reach the river and the route of Walk 28.

Otherwise, turn right onto the pavement of the A4155 passing the 'King's Head' and following the main road for about 350 yards to the corner of a right-hand belt of trees. Here turn right onto path LM13, a farm track alongside the trees with fine views to the right at first towards Flackwell Heath and later on both sides. Follow this track straight on to an old farm site. Bear half left across the corner of this site, then bear half left again onto another track. Just before this track drops steeply, leave it bearing half right across a field to a hedge gap and a signpost near a small tree.

Here cross Winchbottom Lane and go through a gap by a disused gate virtually opposite, then bear half right (still on LM13) heading for the left-hand end of Horton Wood on the skyline. Now continue straight on for half a mile crossing a track, passing left of a ruined cottage called Merton's Hole in its concealed dip and climbing, with fine views of the Thames valley around Bourne End behind, to reach a gate and stile into Monkton Lane alongside the Marlow Bypass. Turn right into Monkton Lane and follow it for quarter of a mile past part of Horton Wood and a right-hand field. On reaching another part of Horton Wood, turn right over a stile onto path LM14 into the wood and follow this waymarked track straight on through this pleasant beechwood for three-quarters of a mile only briefly passing through a plantation and ignoring various tracks and paths to your right. When you finally emerge from the wood at the back of Ray Farm in Winchbottom, the name of which appears to derive from the Old English 'wincel-botm' meaning 'bottom with an angular bend', take a fenced path straight on between the farm and a farm cottage to reach Winchbottom Lane.

Now turn left onto this road and after 100 yards, just before Winchbottom Farm on the right, turn right into a pleasant narrow lane and follow it up the valley bottom into Lower Grounds Wood. In the wood, ignore a branching private road and where the public road ends, take macadam footpath LM22 bearing right, then turn immediately left up a flight of steps to reach Heath End Road by its bridge over the M40. Turn left over this bridge, then, at its far end, turn right into a road signposted to RAF Daws Hill then immediately right again onto a fenced macadam path. This path soon leads you into an old green lane which you follow for a third of a mile disregarding entrances into the RAF base in the former park of Daws Hill House which flanks both sides of the lane. On entering woodland at Keep Hill, take sunken bridleway HW67 straight on downhill, ignoring branching paths to right and left and looking out for ancient earthworks in the form of a hilltop camp to your left. Near the bottom of the hill you reach a macadam track used on your outward route and follow this straight on to Warrenwood Drive. Cross this road bearing half left and retrace your outward route to your starting point.

WALK 21:   Tylers Green

Length of Walk: 5.8 miles / 9.3 Km
Starting Point: Tylers Green village hall.
Grid Ref: SU905938
Maps: OS Landranger Sheets 165 & 175
OS Explorer Sheet 3
(or old Pathfinder Sheet 1138 (SU89/99))
Chiltern Society FP Map No.6
How to get there/Parking: Tylers Green, 3.5 miles
northwest of Beaconsfield, may be reached from the
town by taking the B474 towards Hazlemere for 3.7 miles.
Three-quarters of a mile beyond the 'Crown' at Penn, turn
left into School Road. After quarter of a mile, by the
'Queen's Head', turn right for Tylers Green village hall
about 100 yards along the road on the right. There are
small car parks in front of the village hall and down a
lane opposite.

Tylers Green, which derives its name from the fact that the
local clay soil made it a centre for tilemaking in the Middle
Ages, once played a role in European history, as it was here
that in 1796 Edmund Burke established a school for the
children of French royalist refugees. Historically an outlying
common of High Wycombe, around which a village grew up,
Tylers Green is today scarcely more than a suburb of the town.
Nevertheless the village does retain its attractive green with
its pond and a number of old cottages.

The walk soon leaves this outpost of suburbia behind and
takes you, at first, through peaceful heavily-wooded
countryside by way of the historic Penn House to the
attractive village of Penn Street. It then returns through more
open countryside by way of Winchmore Hill and Penn Bottom
to Tylers Green.

Starting from the entrance to Tylers Green village hall, turn right
onto the road in front of it and follow it to the B474. Turn right onto
this road and follow it for a few yards to the far end of a right-hand
parking bay. Here cross the road and take path P23 along a rough
track opposite. Where the track bears right to a sports ground, follow

an enclosed path beside a left-hand hedge straight on until you enter a field. Here go straight on, passing left of two oak trees, then bear slightly left to the corner of Pugh's Wood. Turn left here onto path P24 entering the wood and ignoring a branching path to your right, then take an obvious path downhill, swinging right round the back of a pit, then left to reach a road. Cross the road, bearing half right, then cross a stile by gates virtually opposite onto path P22 in Common Wood. Here take the right-hand of three paths and follow its defined course straight on through the wood disregarding all branching or crossing tracks for two-thirds of a mile until you eventually reach a stile leading to a road in Penn Bottom.

Turn right onto this road and just before a left-hand bend, turn left over two stiles and follow hedged path P75, soon entering a wood. Some 250 yards into the wood, where the path joins a stony track and Penn House can be glimpsed ahead, follow the track (path P16) straight on, soon leaving the wood and continuing along an avenue of trees in the park of Penn House. Penn House was for centuries the home of the Penn family, a relative of whom, William Penn, founded Pennsylvania. When the male line died out in 1731, it passed through marriage to the Curzon family of Mayfair fame, now the Earls Howe. The house is reputedly where Händel composed part of his 'Messiah'. At an entrance to Penn House, join a macadam drive and follow it straight on. At a junction by Garden Cottage, turn left and continue to follow the drive. Just after a right-hand bend in the drive, turn left over a stile onto path P7 and follow it through the wood to another stile. Cross the stile and bear half right across a field to a concealed stile right of a cottage which leads you onto a road at Penn Street.

Turn left along the road and follow it past the 'Hit or Miss' to a road junction. Here fork left and follow the road across the village green. At a left-hand bend, turn right onto path P77 along the back of the green, passing the cricket pitch and the war memorial to reach a small gate. Continue straight on through the gate and soon join a track. Follow the track straight on to the churchyard gates of Penn Street Church. Built in 1849 by the contemporary Earl Howe, this neo-Gothic church is unusual for the Chilterns in being cross-shaped with a central spire. By the gates, turn right and take path P1 between hedges out to a road. Turn right along the road and, at a right-hand bend, turn left onto path P6 up a drive. By a garage, cross a double stile and follow a left-hand hedge straight on. Where the hedge turns left by a cattle trough, turn right across the field to the corner of another hedge, then follow it straight on until you reach a double stile in it by an electricity pole. Do not cross this stile, but instead bear half left across the field (now on path P3) to a kissing-gate into the right-hand corner of Priestlands Wood. Go through this and follow a fenced path straight on through the wood for quarter of a mile to a kissing-gate into a field. Now bear slightly right across the field to a stile and kissing-gate at the corner of a hedge. Negotiate these and follow a path between hedges straight on to a road at the village of Winchmore Hill.

Here cross the road and keeping right of a hedge, follow the edge of the village green straight on uphill to join a road, then continue straight on along it to a crossroads by the 'Plough Inn'. Here turn right and by the 'Potters Arms' bear slightly right, leaving the road, and follow bridleway P10 across the green, then between a hedge and a wall into a rough lane. Where the lane forks, go right and follow the lane to a road. Cross this road and go through a hedge gap opposite, then take path P12 straight on across the field to enter a strip of woodland just right of a kink in its edge. In the woodland, follow a path straight on to reach a crossing path (P11), then turn left onto it and follow it to a raised macadam drive. Turn left onto this and follow it for some 250 yards. Where the drive bears left and drops down, leave it and go straight on along a path through Branches Wood which gradually bears right. Ignore a branching track to the left (where you join the reverse direction of Walk 25), then leave the wood and follow a grassy track beside a right-hand hedge, later the edge of a wood, winding downhill to reach a road in Penn Bottom.

Turn right along the road and follow it to a road junction. Here turn left and after some 70 yards, turn right onto a rough track (path P25). Where the track forks, leave it and go straight on along a hedged path to a stile into a field. Cross the stile and follow a left-hand hedge, then, where it ends, join a grassy track and follow it straight on for quarter of a mile. After about 200 yards a hedge commences to your left (and you part company with Walk 25), then, just after the second slight left-hand bend in the hedge, by a wide replanted gap in the hedge directly below a copse in the left-hand field, leave the track and bear half right across the field to a hedge gap left of a holly tree in the top corner of the field. Here bear slightly left, joining a track and following it beside a right-hand hedge (now on path P20) to a junction of tracks in a field corner near the fifteenth-century Puttenham Place Farm where you turn left onto path P24. After 75 yards by the corner of a barn, turn right onto path P29 between the barn and a hedge, later following a right-hand fence to join the farm drive. Now follow it to the B474 at Tylers Green. Here cross the main road and take a side-road straight on for quarter of a mile to the 'Queen's Head', then turn right for the village hall.

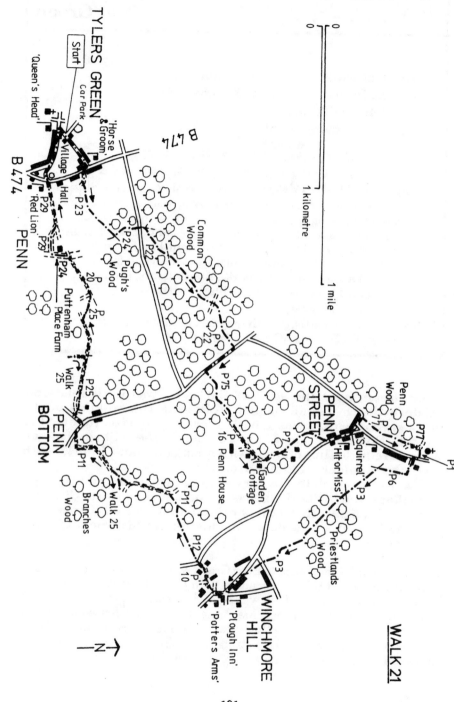

WALK 21

TYLERS GREEN

Start

'Queen's Head'

Car Park

'Horse & Groom'

Village Hall

B474

B474

PENN

'Red Lion'

P29

P29

P23

P24

Pugh's Wood

P22

Common Wood

P24

P20

P25

Puttenham Place Farm

Walk 25

P25

PENN BOTTOM

P11

Branches Wood

Walk 25

P11

P12

P75

16 Penn House

Garden Cottage

PENN STREET

P75

'Squirrel'

'Hit or Miss'

Penn Wood

P77

P6

P3

P1

Priestlands Wood

P3

WINCHMORE HILL

'Plough Inn'

'Potters Arms'

N →

1 kilometre

1 mile

101

WALK 22:   Seer Green

Length of Walk: 5.9 miles / 9.5 Km
Starting Point: Seer Green & Jordans Station.
Grid Ref: SU965910
Maps: OS Landranger Sheet 175 *or* 176
OS Explorer Sheet 3
(or old Pathfinder Sheet 1138 (SU89/99))
(Part only) Chiltern Society FP Maps Nos. 6 & 13
How to get there/Parking: Seer Green & Jordans Station,
1.4 miles east of Beaconsfield, may be reached from the
town by taking the A355 northwards towards Amersham
and turning right onto a road signposted to Seer Green.
Follow this road for 1.3 miles to a right-hand turn
signposted to the station. Turn right here and fork right
again for the station car park. Alternatively, the walk can
be started from Seer Green village, where on-street
parking is possible.
Notes: Heavy nettle growth may be encountered in the
summer on paths SG8, SG22 and CG11.

Seer Green, near the start of the walk, was until relatively
modern times a small hamlet. Following the building of the
railway, however, it has greatly increased in size. Referred to
in the Domesday Book as 'La Sere', the village has an
attractive little flint church with a bellcote, built in 1846, with
a number of older buildings around it.

The walk, which is of a very easy nature, takes you through
the village and visits Hodgemoor Wood. It then skirts Chalfont
St. Giles, passes through parkland at Chalfont Grove and
returns by way of Jordans, famous for its historical Quaker
connections.

Starting from the entrance to Seer Green & Jordans Station, cross the
approach road and take a macadam path (SG1) between the car park
fence and a belt of trees. Follow this, soon turning right, downhill to a
road. Cross the road and continue straight on along a fenced macadam
path (SG1a) uphill to another road. Having crossed this, take a
further macadam path (SG1b) straight on, this time between hedges,
to a road called School Lane at Seer Green. Turn left onto this road

and follow it for over a third of a mile, disregarding all side turnings and passing the 'Jolly Cricketers' and the village church. Just past a garage, turn left into Howard Road. After a few yards, turn right into Howard Crescent and follow it for about 120 yards to a left-hand bend. Here turn right into footpath SG12 between a fence and a wall. At the back of the gardens, the path turns left and later right between fences to a climb-through stile.

Leaving the village behind, cross this stile and bear half left across a field to another stile left of the far corner. Cross this and turn right onto fenced path SG8. On crossing a stile into a field, follow a right-hand fence through two fields passing Big Copse. At the far end of the copse, cross a stile and follow a fenced path straight on to reach Rawlings Lane. Turn right onto this road and follow it for some 300 yards, passing Rawlings Farm to the right which appears to be of sixteenth- or seventeenth- century origin. Having passed a short section of Hodgemoor Wood, at a sharp right-hand bend, cross a stile ahead onto path SG13 into a paddock. Now follow its right-hand hedge to cross a stile, then turn left and follow a left-hand fence to another stile. Cross this and continue straight on between a fence and a hedge to reach a large farm building to your left. Here ignore a footbridge and stile to your right and take path SG22 straight on between a hedge and the building to a stile into Hodgemoor Wood.

Inside the wood, follow a winding path straight on along its edge, passing a number of pits and ignoring branching paths to your left. After quarter of a mile, on reaching a branching path to your right, turn right then immediately left over a stile into a field and take path CG27 following the outside edge of the wood to a hedge gap into the next field. Here turn left and follow the outside edge of the wood to a corner where you turn right ignoring a stile into the wood and continue to follow its outside edge disregarding a second branching path into the wood. Where the wood finally gives way to a left-hand hedge, follow it to where its trees peter out. Here bear half right across the corner of the field to a hedge gap. Go through this and take path CG22 following a left-hand hedge to another stile. Having crossed this, leave the left-hand hedge and continue straight on across a field to a stile about 30 yards left of its far right-hand corner. Cross this and follow a left-hand hedge to a stile into a fenced path, then continue along this path, crossing two further stiles, to reach a road at Three Households on the outskirts of Chalfont St. Giles.

Cross this road, bearing slightly right, and take path CG11 virtually opposite following a right-hand fence and hedge at first, then between hedges. On reaching a golf course, take a fenced path straight on with a hedge to your left at first, later between fences and finally between hedges to leave the golf course at a stile. Having crossed this,

103

continue along a fenced path to enter a belt of trees. Continue straight on through the belt of trees between hedges and fences for some 250 yards until you emerge into a field. Here take a fenced path straight on to enter a tree belt where you ignore a branching path to your right and continue for 40 yards to a gap in the left-hand hedge. Turn left through this gap then bear right across a field to a waymarked hedge gap into a belt of trees ahead. In the tree belt turn left onto a crossing path and follow it out to Narcot Lane.

Here cross this road and turn right along its pavement. Where the pavement ends, cross the road again and continue along its other pavement for a third of a mile, passing a left-hand turn. Having passed a school sign, turn right over a stile onto path CG15 through a belt of trees into a plantation where you follow a right-hand security fence straight on, soon on path CP52. In the trees to the right, you may glimpse Chalfont Grove House, a secret meeting-place for seventeenth-century Quakers. On reaching a gate by the edge of Grove Wood, pass left of it and follow a right-hand fence to reach a stile. Cross this and take path CG14, bearing half right across parkland to a stile into Pond Warren Wood. Having crossed the stile, go straight on through the wood to cross another stile. Now turn left onto path CG16 along the outside edge of the wood to a stile onto a rough macadam drive. Cross the stile, the drive and another stile slightly left of opposite and follow a right-hand hedge to a concealed stile in the corner of the field. Cross this stile and bear half left, following a right-hand fence across a field. By a pond, bear half right and follow a right-hand hedge to a stile. Cross this and follow a path between a hedge and a fence to a bend in a drive, then follow this drive straight on to a road junction at Jordans.

The road to the left leads down to the Meeting House and Mayflower Barn. Both these seventeenth-century buildings were used by the celebrated early Quakers, Penn (founder of Pennsylvania), Penington and Ellwood (friend of the poet, Milton), for their meetings. Mayflower Barn gained its name from a ship's timber used in its construction believed to come from the Mayflower. Cross the major road and follow a road straight on through Jordans village, purpose-built by the Society of Friends in 1919, disregarding all crossing roads and side turnings. Where the road ends, continue straight on down a rough lane into a valley. Here turn left into hedged bridleway SG18 and follow it straight on to a road junction, then continue straight on up the station approach to the station.

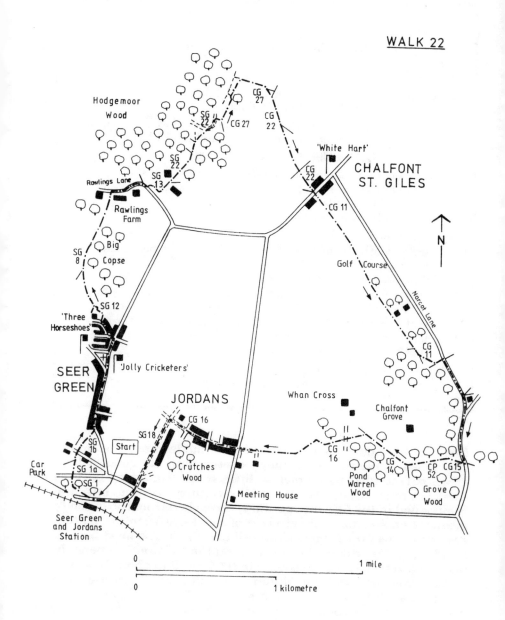

WALK 22

Hodgemoor Wood

CG 27

SG 22

CG 27

CG 22

'White Hart'

CG 22

CHALFONT ST. GILES

SG 22

SG 13

Rawlings Lane

CG 11

Rawlings Farm

SG 8

Big

Copse

N

Golf Course

SG 12

Narcot Lane

'Three Horseshoes'

CG 11

SEER GREEN

'Jolly Cricketers'

JORDANS

Whan Cross

Chalfont Grove

CG 16

SG 18

SG 1b

Start

Crutches Wood

CG 16

CG 14

CP 52

CG 15

Pond Warren Wood

Car Park

SG 1a

SG 1

Grove Wood

Meeting House

Seer Green and Jordans Station

0   1 mile

0   1 kilometre

105

Length of Walk: (A) :   7 miles / 11.2 Km
                          (B) :   2.3 miles / 3.7 Km
                          (C) :   4.5 miles / 7.3 Km

Starting Point: (A/B) Road junction by the 'Crown',
Chalfont St. Giles.
(C) Service road beside A413, 1 mile east
of the centre of Amersham Old Town.

Grid Ref: (A/B) SU990935 / (C) SU973967

Maps: OS Landranger Sheet 176 or Sheets 165 & 175
OS Explorer Sheet 3 (or old Pathfinder Sheet
1138 (SU89/99))
Chiltern Society FP Map No.6

How to get there/Parking: (A/B) Chalfont St. Giles, 3
miles southeast of Amersham Old Town, may be reached
from the town by taking the A413 towards London to the
'Pheasant' roundabout. Here turn right for the village
centre where there is a signposted car park on the right.
(C) From the eastern end of Amersham Bypass, take the
A413 towards London for a third of a mile. Just after a
left-hand bend, turn left into a service road alongside the
A413 where parking is possible.

Notes: Heavy nettle growth may be encountered on path CG29
on Walks A & B in the summer months.

Chalfont St. Giles, despite considerable modern expansion, can
still boast a picturesque village centre with its small village
green surrounded by attractive little shops, cottages and inns.
The church, which is of twelfth-century origin but was
remodelled in the fifteenth century, is reached from the green by
means of an archway beneath part of a sixteenth-century cottage
and is famous for its mediaeval wall paintings. The most notable
building in the village, however, is Milton's Cottage, where the
poet took refuge from the plague in 1665. Built in about 1600, this
cottage was where John Milton completed his 'Paradise Lost'
and it was while he was staying here that Thomas Ellwood, who
had secured the cottage for Milton, is said to have inspired
Milton to write his 'Paradise Regained'.

All three alternative walks explore the attractive section of the Misbourne valley between the Chalfonts and Amersham and offer spectacular views across the valley from the surrounding hills.

Walks A and B start from the road junction by the 'Crown' in the centre of Chalfont St. Giles and take a road called Up Corner, soon becoming Silver Hill, uphill past a green and the 'Fox and Hounds'. After about 300 yards, fork right into Dodds Lane and follow it for quarter of a mile to a crossroads. Here take Hill Farm Lane (path CG28) straight on and follow it uphill, ignoring various entrances to private property. After half a mile, at the top of the hill, just past some farm buildings at the back of Hill Farm, follow the rough road which turns right onto path CG29 and soon ends. Here take an obvious path straight on through scrub to a stile where a view of the Misbourne valley opens out ahead. Cross this stile and take a fenced path beside a right-hand hedge downhill to cross a stile. Now continue along the other side of the hedge to a gate in it. Here bear slightly right to a stile into a belt of trees ahead. Cross this stile and continue straight on to reach a T-junction of paths with the South Bucks Way by the corner of a fence. Here **Walk B** turns right onto path CG30 (now see the last paragraph), while **Walk A** turns left onto path CG30 and follows it, ignoring a branching path to the right, to a stile at the far end of the belt of trees.

Now **Walks A and C** cross this stile and turn right for a few yards to an oak tree. Here turn left, resuming your previous direction, to reach a stile left of an oak tree ahead. Cross this stile and follow a right-hand hedge straight on to a stile into Bottom House Farm Lane with the seventeenth-century Lower Bottom House Farm with its fine timber-framed and weatherboarded buildings to your left and the course of the River Misbourne marked by a line of willows to your right. Cross this road and go through a hedge gap opposite onto path A16, then bear slightly right to a stile in a hedge ahead. Having crossed this, continue straight on, passing close to a bend in the river, to reach the corner of hedge. Here bear slightly left to the corner of a copse, then follow its outside edge to a gate and stile. Cross the stile and follow a right-hand hedge to cross another stile. Now bear slightly left, leaving the hedge and following what is normally a crop-break towards a long red-roofed building at Amersham ahead to reach the corner of a hedge. Here follow a left-hand hedge straight on to a crossing track. Leaving the South Bucks Way, turn right onto this track (path A17) and follow it to a ford and footbridge over the Misbourne. Cross the footbridge and continue to follow the track (now path A17a) to reach the A413. Now cross this main road and turn left onto the service road in front of some houses opposite.

This is the starting point of Walk C. Now **Walks A and C** follow the service road and later a roadside footway beside the A413 towards Amersham for nearly quarter of a mile. Just before reaching another row of houses, turn right down a bank beside a left-hand fence onto path A10 and follow the fence through a field into a wood. Now continue straight on through the wood along the bottom of a dip to reach the A404 by the gates of Stanley Hill Cemetery. Do not join the main road, but turn right onto path A12 left of the cemetery gates and follow it straight on through the wood, ignoring a branching path to the left, to reach a field. In the field, go straight on uphill to the top of the rise with fine views of the Misbourne valley to your right. At the top of the rise, bear half left to a stile just right of where a power-line reaches a hedge ahead. Cross the stile and bear slightly right across a field, heading for a clump of trees right of a single oak tree in the far hedge, to reach a kissing-gate. Go through this and bear half right, following a right-hand hedge with views of Bendrose Grange to your left, to reach a gate and kissing-gate at the end of a line of chestnut trees. Go through the kissing-gate and follow a left-hand hedge to pass through another kissing-gate right of a gate then take path A12a, following a left-hand hedge to a stile into a fenced path which leads you past two large houses to Finch Lane on the edge of Little Chalfont.

Turn right into this rough lane, then immediately turn left over a stile by a gate onto path A14. Now follow a left-hand hedge straight on for a third of a mile to a gate and stile into the end of Coke's Farm Lane, then follow this rough lane straight on to Coke's Lane. Here glance over your left shoulder to see a fine sixteenth-century brick and timber barn at Coke's Farm, then turn right onto the road. After about 200 yards, just past the entrance to 'Thatched House', fork left onto path A15, a fenced path between gardens leading you onto a golf course where a fine view opens out across the Misbourne valley. Here take path CG34 straight on, passing between greens, to enter a corner of Pollards Wood by a white post. In the wood turn right at a waymarked path junction, then, on re-emerging onto the golf course, follow the outside edge of the wood. Where a hedge begins, bear half left re-entering the wood, then, on re-emerging, turn left and immediately left again to re-enter the wood. Where the path eventually leaves the wood again by a green, follow the outside edge of the wood straight on, then, on reaching the edge of a fairway, turn left, continuing to follow the outside edge of the wood over the next rise and down into the next valley. At the bottom of the valley, leave the edge of the wood and follow the valley bottom, keeping right of a sunken gully, an area of scrub and a further sunken gully to reach a gate onto the A413.

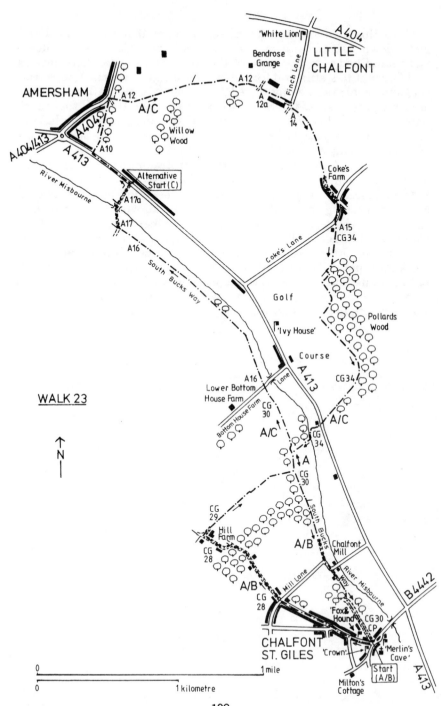

'White Lion'

A404

LITTLE
CHALFONT

Bendrose
Grange

Finch Lane

A404

A12

AMERSHAM

A12

A12a

A/C

A14

A404/413

A404

A10

Willow
Wood

A413

River Misbourne

Alternative
Start (C)

A17a

Coke's
Farm

A17

A15
CG34

A16

South Bucks Way

Coke's Lane

Golf

'Ivy House'

Pollards
Wood

WALK 23

↑
N
—

A16
Lower Bottom
House Farm

Bottom House Farm

Lane

Course

A413

CG34

A/C

CG
30

A/C

CG
34

A

A/C

CG
30

CG
29

Chalfont
Mill

South Bucks

CG
28

Hill
Farm

CG
28

A/B

A/B

Mill Lane

Way

River Misbourne

B4442

'Fox &
Hound'

CG30
CP

CHALFONT
ST. GILES

'Crown'

'Merlin's
Cave'

Start
(A/B)

A413

Milton's
Cottage

0 _____ 1 mile

0 _____ 1 kilometre

109

Cross this road and turn left along its verge, then turn immediately right down a bank and over a stile (still on CG34). Now follow a right-hand hedge to the bank of the River Misbourne, then turn left and follow it to a stile and footbridge. Turn right over the bridge, then continue straight on along the edge of a belt of trees until you reach a crossing path, part of the South Bucks Way. Here **Walk C** turns right onto path CG30 to a stile (now go back three paragraphs), while **Walk A** turns left onto path CG30 and follows it straight on through the belt of trees, ignoring a branching path to the right.

Now **Walks A and B** follow path CG30 straight on through the belt of trees for quarter of a mile. Where the trees eventually peter out, follow a fenced track straight on to reach a bend in Mill Lane. Here go straight on along the road to a left-hand bend, where a detour along the road to the left to the ford past the timber-framed millhouse of Chalfont Mill, reputedly the oldest watermill in the county, is well worthwhile. Otherwise leave the road at the bend and take a rough track (still path CG30) straight on. The rough track soon narrows to a path leading into a copse. In the copse, follow a left-hand fence at first, then gradually bear right to join a wide tree-lined avenue. Now follow it straight on to the village street of Chalfont St. Giles.

WALK 24:　　　　　　　Gerrards Cross

Length of Walk: 9.9 miles / 15.9 Km
Starting Point:　Gerrards Cross Station.
Grid Ref:　TQ002888
Maps:　OS Landranger Sheet 176
　　　　OS Pathfinder Sheets 1139 (TQ09/19) & 1158 (TQ08/18)
How to get there/Parking:　Due to attempts to prevent rail
　commuters blocking residential roads near the station with
　parked cars, parking in this area is a problem. The pay car
　park at the station can be used if space is available or, in
　the afternoons and at weekends, on-street parking is
　possible in Orchehill Avenue and surrounding streets. Either
　can be reached from the junction of the A40 and B416 by
　taking the B416 towards Amersham. After half a mile, on
　crossing the railway bridge, either turn left for the station
　and its car park or go straight on through the town centre,
　then, after a left-hand bend, take the first turning left
　which is Orchehill Avenue and find a suitable place to park.
Notes:　The walk may be muddy in places in wet weather and
　Shire Lane is prone to heavy nettle growth in Summer.

Gerrards Cross today is known as a wealthy commuter-belt
town just outside London, but a mere 100 years ago it
consisted of little more than a few cottages scattered around a
large common. What changed it was the arrival of the railway
in 1906 which gave the village rapid access to London and thus
made it become an attractive rural haven for affluent
Londoners to move to. Despite this, however, modern planning
laws arrived just in time to prevent the town's total absorption
into suburbia and therefore, although motorways have since
been built to the south and east of Gerrards Cross, there are
still a number of surprisingly rural country walks accessible
from the town.

　This particular walk is one of great variety exploring the
valleys of the rivers Misbourne and Colne with their various
lakes and the Grand Union Canal interspersed with crossing
and recrossing the still largely rural ridge separating the two

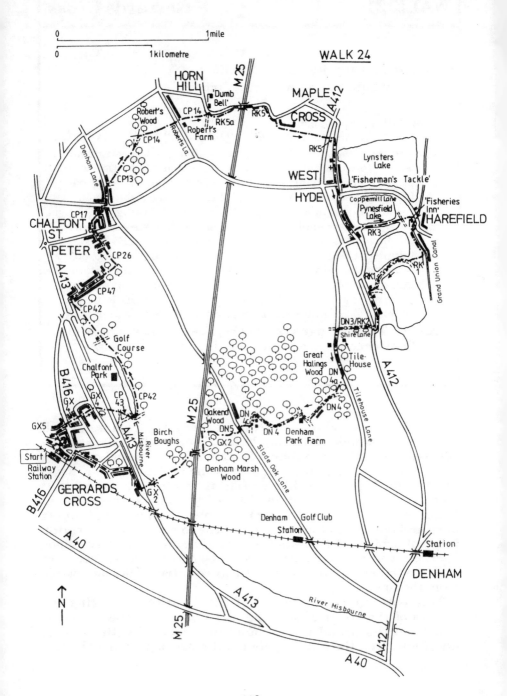

WALK 24

112

valleys where there is a characteristic Chiltern mix of farm-
and woodland. Despite its length, the route is of a generally
easy nature and is ideal for a leisurely day's walk or a long
afternoon in the Summer months.

Starting from the entrance to Gerrards Cross Station, cross its
approach road and take a fenced path opposite uphill. At the top of the
rise, turn sharp right onto footpath GX6a, a winding fenced macadam
alleyway which leads you to a residential road. Turn left onto this
road, then almost immediately turn left again onto path GX5, another
fenced alleyway leading to Orchehill Avenue. Here turn right and
follow this road to the B416. Cross the major road and take a fenced
alleyway (GX4) straight on crossing a further road and continuing to
reach a third road with a belt of trees opposite. Now cross this road
bearing slightly right to take path GX4 through a fence gap virtually
opposite. Follow this obvious path through the belt of trees, then take
path CP43 straight on through scrubland to a stile. Cross this stile
and bear half right onto a sloping path down to the A413, then cross
this dual-carriageway and bear slightly left (still on CP43) to a
concealed stile. Having crossed this stile, bear half right with a fine
view of Chalfont Park, rebuilt by Col. Charles Churchill, brother-in-
law to the eighteenth-century prime minister Horace Walpole, to your
left, to reach a stile onto its drive.
   Cross the stile and drive and a stile opposite, then bear half right
across a field to a stile in the far corner. Cross this and turn left over a
footbridge beside a ford, then follow a lane straight on to cross a
bridge over the River Misbourne near the weir at the outlet of
Chalfont Park Lake. Following restoration work instigated by the
Chiltern Society, this lake has once again become an exceptionally
attractive feature of the local landscape. At the far end of the bridge,
turn left over a stile onto path CP42. Now follow this fenced path near
the shore of the lake for half a mile keeping right at a fork and with
views across the lake in places of Chalfont Park House and its modern
extension. On emerging onto the golf course, continue straight on
following a line of white posts into a clump of trees right of some
sheds. Here cross a macadam track and continue straight on over a
fairway, through a gap in an area of conifers and across another
fairway into a belt of scrub where you eventually emerge over a stile
onto a service road on the edge of Chalfont St. Peter.
   Turn right onto this road and where it turns right and becomes a
private road and public footpath CP47, follow it uphill. Where the
road turns left, leave it and take footpath CP47 straight on between
hedges to a stile, then continue straight on within an avenue of trees.
At the far end of the avenue, cross a stile and turn left onto path CP26

following a left-hand hedge and crossing two stiles to reach a cul-de-sac gravel road. Here continue straight on, soon joining a macadam road called Upway and following it to a T-junction with Joiner's Lane. Turn left onto this road, then immediately right into an alleyway (CP17). On emerging into a cul-de-sac road, follow it to a T-junction, then turn left into Ninnings Road and at a further T-junction, turn right into Copthall Lane.

Now at a staggered crossroads, turn left into Denham Lane, then just before a left-hand bend, turn right onto path CP13, a rough lane. Just before reaching a blue gate, fork left between concrete posts onto a fenced path and follow this to a stile into a field. Bear half right across this field to a stile right of a hawthorn bush and cherry tree, then continue straight on to a stile at the top of a slight rise into Robert's Wood. In the wood, follow an obvious path swinging left and ignoring a branching path to the left, then just past the corner of a field to the right, keep left at the first fork, right at the second and right at the third, passing through holly bushes and dropping into a dip. At the bottom of the dip, turn right onto path CP14, soon leaving the wood by a stile. Now go straight on across a field to a stile in a hedge gap ahead, then continue straight on with views ahead across the Colne valley towards Harefield to reach a stile at the corner of a hedge. Cross this and follow a right-hand hedge straight on to a stile leading to Roberts Lane. Bear slightly left across this road to a stile virtually opposite, then cross this and on entering a paddock, go straight across it to a gate and stile then continue straight on across a field to a gate and stile leading to a bend in a road at the Hertfordshire boundary just outside the hamlet of Horn Hill.

Do not join the road, but cross the entrance to a bridleway and take footpath RK5a bearing slightly right through a belt of trees into a field. Here bear left and follow the belt of trees, later a hedge until you reach a stile onto the road near the M25 bridge. Cross the stile and the bridge and at the far end of the bridge, turn right over another stile onto path RK5, turning immediately left to follow the back of the roadside hedge for quarter of a mile to reach the edge of Maple Cross. Here turn right following a left-hand hedge round the backs of gardens and then continuing downhill to the A412. Cross this road and take a rough lane (still RK5) straight on to reach Old Uxbridge Road just outside West Hyde. Turn right onto this road and follow it straight on for nearly two-thirds of a mile through the most southerly village in Hertfordshire passing the flint Italianate church of St. Thomas of Canterbury and the 'Fisherman's Tackle' and ignoring turnings to right and left. Finally, just past a nursery on the left, turn left onto path RK3, a rough drive which soon narrows to a path and leads you for quarter of a mile between attractive gravel lakes. On reaching a car park, follow its right-hand edge to a macadam road, then cross this and a stile and continue across grassland to a macadam drive and a further stile. Having crossed these, continue straight on to reach Coppermill Lane by a bridge over the River Colne on the edge of Harefield.

Turn right onto this road crossing the bridge and passing the 'Fisheries Inn', then turn right by the pub onto the Grand Union Canal towpath. Follow the towpath for quarter of a mile, then after crossing a hump-backed bridge, turn right through a gap onto path RK1 following the bank of a stream through a marsh to reach a footbridge. Cross this bridge, then turn right onto a rough road between the stream and a large lake. Follow this for over a third of a mile until you enter a sand store, then at the far side of it, turn right over two bridges by the mill-race at Troy Mill to reach Old Uxbridge Road. Turn left onto this road and follow it for quarter of a mile passing between bollards at one point, then at the far end, pass right of a mound to join the A412.

Here cross the A412 and turn right, then immediately left onto RK2/DN3, a bridleway known as Shire Lane. This green lane leads you uphill on the county boundary, later with fine views to your right along the Colne valley towards Rickmansworth, to reach Tilehouse Lane. Turn left onto this road and follow it for a third of a mile passing the grounds of Tile House with their fine redwoods and cedars. On entering Great Halings Wood, which in June is ablaze with rhododendron blossom, turn right after 100 yards over a stile onto path DN4a and follow this ill-defined winding path through the wood to reach a stile into Halings Lane (DN4). Turn right onto this macadam road and where its surface ends, take a rough lane straight on. At a T-junction of lanes turn right passing Denham Park Farm to your left, then at a fork keep left and follow a rough winding lane for nearly half a mile, entering woodland, passing three large ponds and then turning left. After the lane becomes macadamed, just before a hydrant and the drive to 'Blackbush', turn right onto a narrow woodland path (DN4c) following a mossy boundary bank. On reaching a chestnut paling fence, cross the left-hand ditch and continue along its other side to reach Slade Oak Lane.

Turn left onto this road and just before a bend, turn right onto path DN5 following a left-hand fence into Oakend Wood. Where the fence ends, take path GX2 straight on through the woods to reach the M25 fence. Here turn left and follow the fence to a footbridge over the motorway, then turn right over this bridge. At the far end, turn left to reach a gate, but do not go through it. Instead turn right to follow a fenced path along a belt of trees to a stile. Cross this and follow a fenced path downhill along the edge of a wood called Birch Boughs with views of the Misbourne valley ahead. Near the bottom corner of the wood, cross a stile into a field and follow a right-hand hedge downhill through two fields to cross two footbridges over the River Misbourne and a backwater. Now follow a right-hand ditch to a stile onto the A413. Here cross the dual-carriageway to reach a side road, turn right onto it and take the second turning left (Oak End Way). Follow this road uphill for nearly half a mile to reach Packhorse Road. Turn left onto this and just before the railway bridge, turn right for the station.

WALK 25:   Beaconsfield Station

Length of Walk: 7.5 miles / 12.1 Km

Starting Point: Entrance to north side of Beaconsfield Station.

Grid Ref: SU940912

Maps: OS Landranger Sheet 175
OS Explorer Sheet 3 (or old Pathfinder Sheet 1138 (SU89/99))
Chiltern Society FP Maps Nos. 6 & 13

How to get there/Parking: From the junction of the A40 and B474 in Beaconsfield Old Town, take the B474 northwards for three-quarters of a mile to Beaconsfield Station. Here car parks are available at the Station and behind Waitrose.

Notes: Heavy nettle growth may be encountered on path P17 in summer.

Beaconsfield Station was opened in 1906 as part of the Great Western and Great Central Joint Railway, the last main line to be built into London. At the time, it was to the north of the town, but the coming of the railway, which enabled rapid travel into London and caused a decline in importance of the old coach road, also soon resulted in mushrooming housing development around the station and so today it is the New Town around the railway station rather than the Old Town on the A40 which forms the commercial centre of Beaconsfield. Although the New Town has few historic buildings, it does have one place of interest in the form of the Bekonscot Model Village with its extensive model railway and miniature buildings and landscape, all at a scale of 1 : 12, which was created many years ago in a large garden.

The walk soon leaves the New Town behind and explores the unspoilt Penn Country to the north with its high ridges, deep valleys and extensive woodland, visiting Forty Green and the picturesque hilltop village of Penn and skirting Winchmore Hill and Coleshill before returning to Beaconsfield.

Starting from the entrance to the north side of Beaconsfield Station, take the approach road westwards to reach Station Road (B474). Here turn right to a roundabout, then take the second turning off it (Reynolds Road) and follow it to a bend. Now leave the road and take enclosed path B1 straight on. At a junction of paths, bear half left and continue for some 250 yards to a further junction. Here turn right, then fork left (still on path B1) to reach a macadam drive. Bear right onto this to reach a cul-de-sac road, then turn left to a road junction. Here turn right, then fork immediately left into an alleyway (still B1) and follow this, crossing three further roads and becoming path P49, eventually reaching a gate and stile into Hogback Wood. Cross the stile and go straight on downhill through the wood into a field and up again to reach a stile near a barn. Having crossed this, follow a right-hand fence to reach a road near the telephone box in Forty Green. This small hamlet is principally known for its ancient inn, the 'Royal Standard of England', which is believed to have been renamed thus in the late seventeenth century to mark its use as a refuge and temporary headquarters by King Charles I during the Civil War.

Turn left onto the road and, at a bend, turn right into a rough lane uphill past some cottages to reach a stile by double gates at the top end of the lane. Cross the stile and take path P36 straight on across a field to a stile by gates, then bear slightly left to two further stiles leading into Saunder's Wood. Inside the wood, bear left and at a fork, bear left again onto path P39. Now follow the inside edge of the wood, ignoring a branching path to the left, then take path P38 straight on, still following the inside edge of the wood into Corker's Wood, a mature beechwood. On eventually leaving the wood near large gates, take a macadam private road straight on with glimpses of Penn Church between the trees ahead. After a third of a mile, shortly after passing brick buildings to the right concealing Penbury Grove, where the left-hand fence turns away to the left, turn left onto path P37 following it with fine views to your left over the hills to the south towards the Thames valley and Maidenhead. Now follow a left-hand hedge straight on past a large house to a stile in a corner of the field leading to a narrow lane called Paul's Hill. Turn right onto this road and follow it uphill into Penn, where the fourteenth-century church is to your left and picturesque seventeenth-century brick-and-flint cottages with climber roses are to your right.

At the junction with the B474, turn right onto it, passing the seventeenth-century 'Crown', then, at the far end of its car park, turn left over a stile onto path P17 into a field, where a fine view opens out across Penn Bottom towards Winchmore Hill and Coleshill. Now follow a left-hand wooden fence round the side and rear of the pub car park, before turning right to reach two stiles into Vicarage Wood. In the wood, follow an obvious waymarked path straight on, forking left at one point, to reach and cross a stile where there is a fine view of the remote Penn Bottom. Now bear slightly left, following a crop-break towards an indentation in the edge of the wood ahead, downhill to a grassy track in the valley bottom. Turn right onto this track (path P25), joining the reverse direction of Walk 21. Where the track doglegs to the right and a hedge commences, leave the track and follow the left side of the hedge to a stile. Cross this and continue straight on between hedges to emerge at a track junction, then take a track straight on to reach a road.

Turn left onto this road and at a road junction, turn right. After about 100 yards, turn left through a hedge gap onto path P11. Now follow a grassy track winding uphill along the edge of a wood, then beside a left-hand hedge to enter Branches Wood. At a fork in the wood, go right onto path P13 (leaving Walk 21), then, on reaching a macadam private road, bear half right across it and take a woodland path straight on leading to a stile into a plantation. Cross the stile and go straight on through the plantation to reach a stile emerging by a large pit. Walk round the left side of the pit and then go straight on across a field to the left-hand of two hedge gaps leading onto a road about 30 yards left of a tall oak. Cross the road and a stile opposite into fenced path P26 along the edge of an overgrown orchard. At the far end of the orchard, cross a stile and follow a right-hand hedge straight on to reach a copse. Here turn right over a stile, then turn left past the copse and turn left again through a hedge gap. Now follow a left-hand hedge to the far end of the field. Here turn right over two stiles into a paddock, then turn left onto path P14 crossing the paddock to a stile by the right-hand end of a hedge. Cross this and bear slightly left across the field to a stile onto a road on the edge of Winchmore Hill.

Turn right onto this road and follow it downhill, then, by a fine timber-framed house called 'Lowlands', take a rising grass track on the left to reach a concealed stile in the left-hand hedge. Turn left over this stile onto path P86 and follow it uphill beside a right-hand hedge to a stile leading to a road near a junction. Turn right onto this road, then, at the junction, turn right again and follow the road downhill. At the beginning of a double-bend by Hertfordshire House (so named because the parish of Coleshill was, until 1832, a detached enclave of Hertfordshire where seventeenth-century Quakers often took refuge from the Bucks justices), turn left over a stile by a gate onto path CO11. Now cross a field diagonally to a gate and stile in the far corner. Cross this stile and follow a fenced grassy track uphill to pass through a kissing-gate by a gate near Lucking's Farm. Bear slightly right across a paddock to another kissing-gate, then follow a left-hand hedge straight on, ignoring a gate and kissing-gate in it, until you reach the edge of a wood. Do not enter the wood, but turn right onto path CO10 following its outside edge. At the far end of the wood, bear slightly right, following a left-hand hedge into a second field, then turn left onto a path into a wood. Just inside the wood, fork left onto a waymarked path through mature beechwoods, winding its way downhill into the valley bottom.

At a T-junction with a track (bridleway B8), turn left onto it and follow it until you reach a crossways by the corner of a field to your right. Here turn right onto fenced bridleway B6 and follow it uphill, soon leaving the woods behind and reaching a macadam farm road at the top. Turn right, briefly joining this road, then, by gates leading to a cottage, bear slightly right, leaving the road, passing through a kissing-gate and crossing two sets of rails onto path B4 entering Great Beard's Wood. After some 200 yards, at a fork, bear half left onto a waymarked path entering a plantation. At a second fork by the corner of a fence, bear half right, descending gradually to reach a waymarked path junction. Here cross a stile and turn left onto path P64, following a left-hand boundary bank along the edge of a mature beechwood. At a path junction, go straight on over a boundary bank into mature beechwoods and continue to follow a left-hand boundary bank, ignoring branching paths to the right. By the rear corner of some gardens, bear slightly left onto path B3, following a right-hand wire-mesh fence. Where the path forks, go straight on between fences through an oakwood. At one point, the left-hand fence ends, but soon resumes, then the woods gradually give way to gardens and you emerge into Ledborough Lane.

Turn right along this road, then, just before its junction with Sandelswood End, turn left onto the tree-lined macadam path B40. On reaching a road called St. Michael's Green, follow it straight on past the church of St. Michael and All Angels to a T-junction. Here turn right into Caledon Close and at its end, take a fenced path off the left side of the loop road to reach Beaconsfield Station.

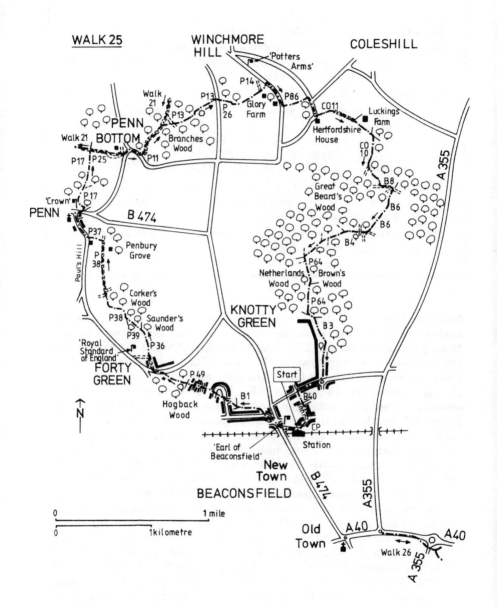

WALK 25

WINCHMORE HILL

COLESHILL

'Potters Arms'

P14

P86

P13

Walk 21

P13

P26

Glory Farm

CO11

Luckings Farm

PENN BOTTOM

Walk 21

Branches Wood

Hertfordshire House

CO 10

P17 P25

P11

B8

'Crown'

P17

Great Beard's Wood

B6

PENN

B474

B6

P37

B4

Penbury Grove

P64

Paul's Hill

P38

Netherlands Wood

Brown's Wood

Corker's Wood

P64

P38

Saunder's Wood

KNOTTY GREEN

B3

P39

P36

'Royal Standard of England'

FORTY GREEN

P49

Start

B40

B1

Hogback Wood

N

CP

'Earl of Beaconsfield'

Station

New Town

BEACONSFIELD

A355

A355

B474

0 ————— 1 mile

0 ————— 1 kilometre

Old Town

A40

A40

Walk 26

A355

121

WALK 26: Beaconsfield (Old Town)

Length of Walk: 8.7 miles / 14.0 Km

Starting Point: Mini-roundabout at junction of A40 (London End) & northbound A355 by the entrance to Wilton Park, Beaconsfield Old Town.

Grid Ref: SU948902

Maps: OS Landranger Sheet 175 (or 176 except 200 yards at start/finish)
OS Explorer Sheet 3 (or old Pathfinder Sheets 1138 (SU89/99) & 1157 (SU88/98))
(part only) Chiltern Society FP Map No.13

Parking: Numerous parking spaces are available in London End (A40) or, if full, ample additional spaces can be found in Windsor End near the Church.

Notes: Heavy nettle growth may be encountered in summer, particularly on path B48.

Beaconsfield Old Town with its profusion of picturesque sixteenth- and seventeenth-century houses, shops and inns is the epitome of the old Buckinghamshire market town. In 1909, Beaconsfield so captivated the poet, G.K. Chesterton that he decided to move there from London and spent the remaining twenty-seven years of his life living in the town. Three centuries earlier, another poet came to Beaconsfield when Edmund Waller and his mother bought Hall Barn, a large mansion just outside the town, while in 1769 the political theorist, Edmund Burke, bought the Gregories Estate as a country retreat. Both Waller and Burke lie buried at the heavily-restored fifteenth-century parish church near the roundabout marking the centre of the Old Town.

The walk first has to take you over or under the major new roads which have relieved Beaconsfield of some of its traffic burden, before reaching surprisingly remote and well-wooded Chiltern countryside and the unspoilt village of Hedgerley, which is a mere 20 miles from Central London. From here you recross the M40 and continue across the spacious Bulstrode Park to skirt Gerrards Cross before returning through more quiet and heavily-wooded Chiltern countryside to Old Beaconsfield.

Starting from the mini-roundabout at the junction of the A40 (London End) and the northbound A355 by the entrance to Wilton Park, take the right-hand pavement of the A40 eastwards. On approaching a large roundabout, where the footway ends, fork right onto path B44, following the old line of the road to an underpass under the A355. Here go through a fence gap and follow a fenced path through the right-hand side of the underpass. At its far end, bear right onto a fenced path, crossing a stile and continuing through a tree belt to a stile onto Pyebush Lane. Turn right onto this road and follow it for nearly a third of a mile until you reach the end of the road. Here go straight on over a stile onto path B48 and follow this fenced path to the M40 fence, where it turns sharp left and continues alongside the motorway for near half a mile to reach a flight of steps leading up to a bridge. Turn right over this bridge, then cross a road and a stile by a gate opposite onto path HE19 which follows the edge of the field straight on. Just past some cottages to the right, at the corner of a hedge, bear half left across the field, passing left of an oak tree to reach a corner of Cave Wood. Here bear slightly left along the outside edge of the wood to enter the wood in a corner of the field. Cross this and follow an obvious woodland track straight on downhill to a macadam farm road. Turn right onto this road and after some 30 yards, turn left onto a woodland track. Where this track turns right, leave it and follow a path straight on, eventually crossing a stile and soon reaching a road.

Turn right onto this and after about 80 yards, turn left over a stile by a gate onto path HE5. Now bear half right across the field to a hedge gap by a telegraph pole right of Sutton's Wood, then go straight on across two further fields, with a view to your right of Mount Pleasant Farm with its seventeenth-century timber-framed farmhouse, to a gate and stile by the corner of Sutton's Wood. Cross the stile and bear left, following the outside edge of the wood with a view across the valley to Hedgerley's attractive church. At the far end of the wood, follow a sporadic left-hand hedge along the top of a steep bank, bearing right, then, where the hedge ends, bear half left across a field to a stile in the corner leading to Hedgerley village street.

Hedgerley, formerly a centre for brickmaking as witnessed by the name of one of its pubs and traces of old claypits, has somehow escaped the suburbanisation which has afflicted most villages so close to London and remains a real picture-book country village. Its church was, in fact, only built in 1852 to replace an earlier building which was demolished, but it contains a number of relics from the earlier building including a piece of seventeenth-century velvet, reputed to be the remains of a cloak given to the church by King Charles II as an altar cloth. Other buildings are, however, older including 'Old

Quaker's House', a timber-framed sixteenth-century building.

Turn right along the village street, passing 'Old Quaker's House' and the 'White Horse'. Just past a left-hand duckpond shaded by fine willows, turn left by Court Farm into a lane (path HE13), where you join the route of Walk 29. Now follow this out of the village to a gate and stile near a corner of Church Wood. Here cross this stile and, parting company with Walk 29, follow the outside edge of Church Wood through two fields. Now take a grass track across a third field to a gate and stile. Cross the stile and follow a left-hand fence to a gate and kissing-gate leading to the M40 underpass. At the far end of the underpass, go through a kissing-gate and take path GX23, following a left-hand fence straight on to a gate and stile leading to a road. Turn right onto this road and follow it to a right-hand bend, then fork left onto path GX15, going straight on between large brick gateposts into Bulstrode Park. Legend has it that this name arose because Shobington, the Saxon who owned the park at the time of the Norman conquest, and his men routed the Norman troops sent to dispossess him thanks to being mounted on bulls! In the park, follow a metalled track straight on to a gate and kissing-gate, then bear slightly right off the track onto a worn path leading you to a stile. Cross this and bear slightly right, following a worn path towards a distant house at Gerrards Cross for nearly half a mile to reach a kissing-gate into the end of a cul-de-sac road. Follow this road past the entrances to 'Blue Cedars' and 'Maple Downs', then turn left onto a path between a hedge and a fence (still GX15) and follow it between gardens to the A40 on the edge of Gerrards Cross.

Cross this road and turn left along its pavement, then turn immediately right onto path GX8 down some concealed steps into a copse. Follow the obvious path through the copse, then a fenced path along the edge of a field, eventually emerging at a road junction. Here turn left and follow the road straight on for a third of a mile, crossing the railway. Where the road forks, turn left into Maltmans Lane and follow it for 300 yards, rounding a right-hand bend. At a second right-hand bend, turn left through a kissing-gate onto path CP31, following a fenced path past a large new house to reach a kissing-gate. Go through this, turn right onto a macadam farm road and follow it for about 200 yards. On nearing Parkwood Farm, fork right onto a fenced path, going through a hedge gap and along the edge of a field. By farm buildings, bear slightly left, rejoining the macadam road, then, where the road turns right into a farmyard, go straight on through a squeeze-stile and follow a fenced path to a junction. Here continue straight on through a kissing-gate and follow a hedged path to a kissing-gate and road at Layter's Green.

Turn left onto the road, then immediately right onto a track into a

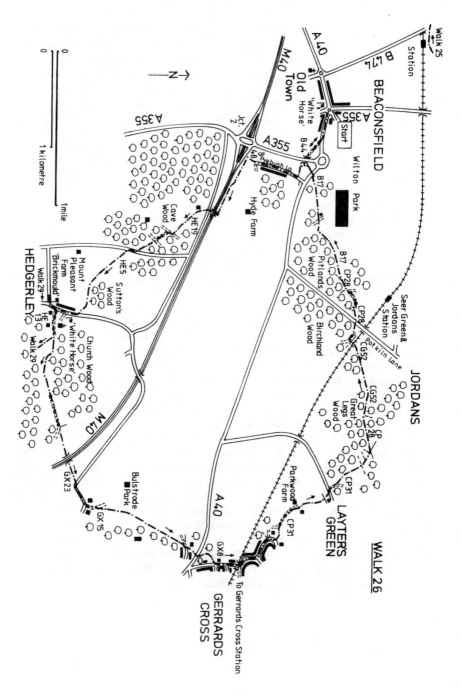

WALK 26

125

wood (still on path CP31). Follow this track straight on, ignoring a branching track to the right and passing through a kissing-gate. Now take a fenced path straight on, soon passing along the edge of a field. At the far end of the field, disregard a crossing path and bear slightly left onto a path dropping gently through the wood. Ignore branching paths to the left and at the far side of the wood, turn left onto path CP28 running along its inside edge. Soon you leave the right-hand field behind and continue straight on through Great Legs Wood, ignoring any branching paths, crossing a stile under a powerline and dropping past a pit two stiles at the edge of the wood (now on path CG52). Here follow a left-hand hedge straight on, with a view towards Jordans to your right, to reach another stile, then follow a left-hand fence straight on through two fields, passing a copse and continuing to a white kissing-gate leading to a railway crossing. Now take path CP28 again, crossing the railway carefully and passing through a kissing-gate, then bear half right onto a track between a thicket and a plantation. After some 60 yards, fork left onto a narrow path through the plantation into mature woodland and follow it straight on to a stile into Potkiln Lane.

Cross this road and a stile opposite and bear half left to a corner of Pitlands Wood by a pylon. Here bear half left again and follow the outside edge of the wood to a stile in a corner of the field. Cross this stile and go straight on into the wood initially under a powerline. After some 150 yards, bear slightly right away from the powerline, soon reaching a kissing-gate into Wilton Park. Now take path B17, following a left-hand fence soon with a playing field to your right. At the far end of the wood to your left, bear half left across grassland to a corner of a fence by a large oak, then bear half left again, initially following a left-hand fence but then bearing away through bushes on an obvious path to join a right-hand fence. On reaching a macadam drive, cross it and continue straight on behind garages to a footbridge and two stiles. Cross these and go straight on across an old parkland field to a hedge gap under a powerline, then bear slightly left across the next field to a stile in the A40 fence. Cross this and turn right along the bottom of the embankment to a flight of steps, then turn left up the steps to the A40. Now cross this dual-carriageway carefully and take a macadam path (still B17) straight on to reach the entrance to the A355 underpass. Here turn right onto path B44 through the underpass and retrace your steps into Beaconsfield.

WALK 27:   Wooburn Green

Length of Walk: 6.1 miles / 9.8 Km

Starting Point: Public car park in Red Lion Way,
   Wooburn Green.

Grid Ref: SU912885

Maps: OS Landranger Sheet 175
   OS Explorer Sheet 3 (or old Pathfinder Sheet
   1157 (SU88/98))
   (part only) Chiltern Society FP Map No.13

How to get there/Parking: Wooburn Green, 2.2 miles
   southwest of Beaconsfield, may be reached from High
   Wycombe by taking the A40 towards London to Knaves
   Beech Roundabout (M40 Junction 3) then taking the
   A4094 towards Wooburn Green, Bourne End and
   Maidenhead. Follow this for 1.5 miles to a large village
   green on the left, then turn right onto a road signposted to
   Flackwell Heath. Now turn right again into Red Lion Way
   where a free car park is on your right. (This is not to be
   confused with the 'Red Lion' car park.)

Notes: Heavy nettle growth may be encountered in summer,
   particularly on path B19 and parts of the walk tend to be
   boggy.

Wooburn Green, although now linked by continuous
development to High Wycombe, has managed to preserve some
of its village character. Set around a well-kept green, the
village which was once known as 'Bishop's Wooburn', has a
number of attractive inns and cottages, some of which date
from the seventeenth century. The River Wye, with its willows,
flows past the village and there are green hills on both sides of
the valley.

The walk itself crosses the Wye and scales the ridge to the
east, makes a wide circle on the surprisingly remote hilltop
plateau taking in the hamlet of Burghers Hill and Littleworth
Common and a variety of pleasant countryside in between,
and then drops back down into Wooburn Green.

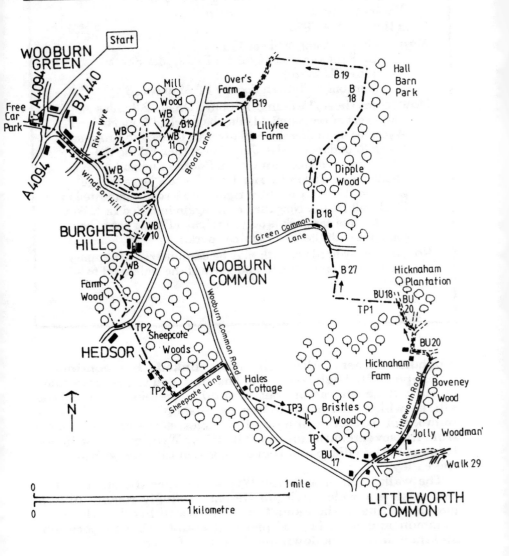

WALK 27

WOOBURN GREEN

Start

Free Car Park

A4094

B4440

River Wye

Windsor Hill

Mill Wood

WB 12

WB 24

WB 11

B19

Over's Farm

B19

Broad Lane

Lillyfee Farm

B19

B 18

Hall Barn Park

Dipple Wood

B18

Green Common Lane

WB 23

WB 10

BURGHERS HILL

WB 9

Farm Wood

WOOBURN COMMON

Wooburn Common Road

B 27

TP1

BU18

BU 20

Hicknham Plantation

BU 20

TP2

Sheepcote Woods

HEDSOR

TP2

Sheepcote Lane

Hales Cottage

TP3

Bristles Wood

TP 3

BU 17

Hicknham Farm

Littleworth Road

Boveney Wood

'Jolly Woodman'

Walk 29

N

0 _____ 1 mile

0 _____ 1 kilometre

LITTLEWORTH COMMON

128

Starting from the entrance to the public car park in Wooburn Green, turn left into Red Lion Way, then left again down Whitepit Lane to the A4094. Cross this and go straight across the green into Windsor Lane, a road leaving the green on the far side. Follow the road out of the village, crossing the River Wye by a narrow humpbacked bridge. At a sharp right-hand bend, turn left up some steps onto path WB23 to enter a field. Now bear right and follow the hedge uphill to cross a stile into Mill Wood. Here continue parallel to the road but do not join it until reaching a road junction at the top of Windsor Hill. Turn right here, crossing the top of the hill road and entering bridleway WB10 between a fence and a hedge to the left of the entrance to a private road called The Chase. Follow this bridleway straight on, eventually crossing The Chase and passing between buildings into the end of the village street at Burghers Hill (formerly known as Beggars Hill).

Follow this narrow road through the hamlet to a sharp left-hand bend. Turn right here onto bridleway WB9, passing a gabled cottage whose upper storey juts out across the bridleway in a fashion most perilous to horseriders! Just beyond this, turn left and follow the fenced bridleway along the edge of Farm Wood. After some 200 yards, disregarding a crossing path, bear half left into the wood. Now follow the bridleway, ignoring two branches to the left and then crossing a clearing, to reach a bridlegate leading to a road near Hedsor Rectory, onto which you turn left. At a left-hand bend, turn right into bridleway TP2 between a hedge and the edge of Sheepcote Woods. After quarter of a mile, by a cottage, the bridleway joins a drive and follows it out to Sheepcote Lane. Turn left along this road to a junction, then turn right into Wooburn Common Road. Just past Hales Cottage, at a left-hand bend, turn left onto path TP3 between the garden hedge and a copse. On leaving the copse by a stile, go straight on beside a hedge. After quarter of a mile, cross a stile and continue straight on, keeping left of a hedge on what soon becomes a fenced path along the outside edge of Bristles Wood. After a third of a mile, this path (now BU17) leads you to Littleworth Road at Littleworth Common.

Turn left onto this road and follow it for nearly half a mile, ignoring two turnings to the right and passing Dropmore's Victorian church and the 'Jolly Woodman'. At a right-hand bend in a dip in the road, fork left up path BU20. In a few yards, turn left onto the drive to Hicknaham Farm. By the farm, turn right along a rough lane, forking left of Hicknaham Plantation. Just past a belt of trees on the left, turn left over a stile by a gate onto path BU18 (later TP1), following a fence across a field. On reaching a hedge, turn right over a stile and follow the hedge (later on path B27) until you reach a road called Green Common Lane.

Go straight on along this road, soon bearing left. About 100 yards beyond this bend, by a holly tree, turn right over a stile onto path B18, following a line of fence posts across a field to a stile into a corner of Dipple Wood. Follow an obvious path straight on through the wood to emerge through a gap into a field. Now follow the outside edge of the wood, crossing a stile at the first field boundary and passing through a hedge gap at the second. Halfway across the third field, turn left onto path B19 passing left of an oak tree to reach the right-hand of two hedge gaps in the far corner. Go through this and keep straight on across another field to a hedge gap into a narrow green lane, some 50 yards right of the right-hand end of a belt of low trees. Turn left into this lane and follow it for some 350 yards passing Over's Farm and emerging into a narrow road.

Cross the road and a stile and go diagonally across a field to a stile into Broad Lane left of the centre of Mill Wood ahead. Here cross the road and take bridleway B19 into the wood, following it (later WB11) for some 200 yards, until reaching a T-junction with a crossing path. Turn left here and after passing between holly bushes, turn right onto path WB12, then fork immediately left onto path WB24 and follow this downhill, ignoring two crossing tracks and reaching a stile into a field. Bear half left across the field to a stile. Cross this and continue straight on across the next field to a redundant stile, descending a slope and steps onto Windsor Hill. From here you retrace your steps to Wooburn Green.

Length of Walk: (A) 8.0 miles / 12.8 Km
                                (B) 5.7 miles / 9.1 Km

Starting Point: Car park by Bourne End Public Library.

Grid Ref: SU894875

Maps: OS Landranger Sheet 175 ˙
             OS Explorer Sheet 3 (or old Pathfinder Sheet
             1157 (SU88/98))
             Chiltern Society FP Maps Nos. 1 & 13 &
             East Berks RA Group FP Map No.2

How to get there/Parking: Bourne End, 4 miles north of
    Maidenhead, may be reached from the town by taking the
    A4094 northwards. In Bourne End, fork left onto the
    A4155 to the Shopping Parade, where a car park is
    signposted to the right.

Bourne End, although it has existed since at least the thirteenth
century, has only developed from a hamlet into a small town in
relatively modern times. Situated near the confluence of the
River Thames and the Wye, which flows through High
Wycombe, Bourne End's principal attraction is the river and it
is one of the most popular locations for sailing on the river.

   Both walks follow the Thames towpath along the beautiful
stretch of river between Bourne End and the Marlow Bypass,
against the magnificent backdrop of Winter Hill. The routes
then cross the river and climb through Quarry Wood to the
ridge of Winter Hill, where panoramic views of the Thames
Valley can be obtained, before dropping down onto Cock
Marsh, from which Walk B returns direct to Bourne End, while
Walk A returns by way of the picturesque village of Cookham.

Both walks start from the car park by Bourne End Public Library and
take Wakeman Road out to the Shopping Parade. Here cross the
A4155 and take Wharf Lane opposite, bearing right, and follow it to a
road junction with a small traffic island with a tree on it. Bear slightly
left here, still on Wharf Lane, to reach a railway level-crossing. Here
take path WB5b straight on over the level-crossing into a boatyard to
reach the Thames towpath. Turn right onto this (path WB5, later LM1)
and follow it along the riverbank for nearly half a mile until you leave

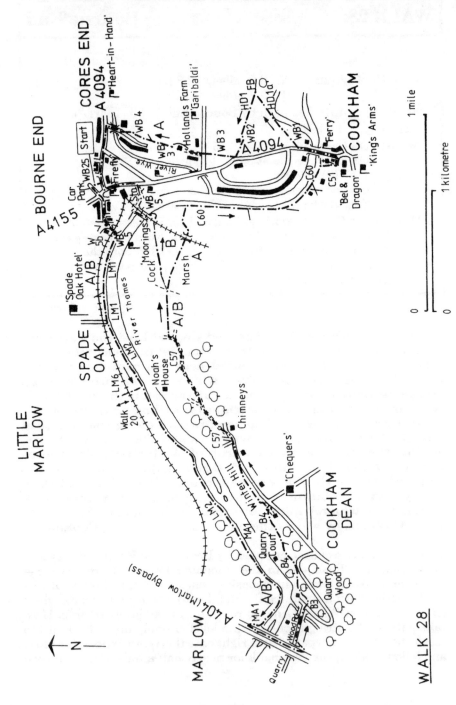

LITTLE MARLOW

A BOURNE END

A4155

CORES END
A 4094

'Heart-in-Hand'

'Spade Oak Hotel'

SPADE OAK

Start

Car Park

'Fireflies'

River Wye

River Thames

Walk 20

Noah's House

Chimneys

Cock Moorings

Marsh

Holland's Farm

'Garibaldi'

A 4094

'King's Arms'

Ferry

'Bel & Dragon'

COOKHAM

Winter Hill

'Chequers'

COOKHAM DEAN

Quarry Court

Quarry Wood

MARLOW

A 404 (Marlow Bypass)

←N—

1 mile

1 kilometre

0

WALK 28

the built-up area at a small car park at Spade Oak Wharf, site of a former ferry. Cross the car park and follow the towpath (now LM2, later MA1) for a further two miles, passing the end of Walk 20 at the beginning of the second field.

Eventually Marlow Bypass Bridge is reached. Here turn right along the near side of the bridge to reach and climb a flight of steps to the Bypass. At the top, step over the crash-barrier and turn left over the bridge, crossing the river with views to the right of the picturesque riverside town of Marlow. After quarter of a mile, on crossing a further bridge over Quarry Wood Road, turn left onto a flight of steps and descend to this road. Turn right along the road and follow it until it crosses a bridge over a stream into Quarry Wood. At a road junction here, leave the road and take a woodland path (B3) straight on, soon bearing left and climbing gently up a terraced path across the face of the hill. Near the top, the path bears right and climbs more steeply, eventually going up steps to a road. Do not join the road, but bear left onto path B4, another terraced path behind the roadside crash-barrier, following the contours of the hill through the wood. In places, extensive views open out through the trees across Marlow and the Thames Valley to the hills above High Wycombe. Ignore a branching path to the right and after third of a mile, join a drive, then, after about 20 yards, turn left onto a path through a belt of scrub into a hilltop car park at Winter Hill with panoramic views of the Thames Valley.

Here cross a small bank on the left of the car park to take the upper of two paths along the hilltop and then follow it until scrub forces you to join the road. At a road junction, go straight on, then just past a large red-brick house with security gates, turn left onto a track (path C57). Follow this downhill, ignoring lesser branching tracks, to reach Cock Marsh. Here follow the track, turning left to a gate, but do not go through this gate. Instead turn right and follow a fence and hawthorn hedge along the edge of the marsh, a National Trust property. Where the hedge and fence turn left, **Walk A** bears half right across the marsh to a bridge under the Bourne End railway near two double-pole electricity pylons. Now omit the next paragraph.

Walk B now goes straight on across the marsh to a gate and stile right of an electricity pole right of the last in a row of bungalows. Here go under a railway bridge, turn left over a stile by a gate and follow a left-hand hedge to the bank of the Thames. Now turn left onto the Thames towpath (C60) passing through a kissing-gate and under a railway bridge, then turn left up a flight of steps to cross a footbridge over the Thames on the side of the railway bridge. At the far end of the bridge descend some steps, go through a gate and turn right onto fenced path WB5. On reaching the end of a gravel lane, bear left and follow it, ignoring a branching path to your right, to reach the A4155.

Turn left onto this, passing Bourne End's Victorian church and the railway station to reach a mini-roundabout. Here turn right then immediately left onto fenced bridleway WB25 right of Lloyds Bank's car park to reach your starting point.

Walk A now goes under the bridge, crossing a stile at each side, then bears left for a few yards to avoid a drainage channel. As soon as possible bear right across the marsh to join the Thames towpath (path C60). Turn right onto this and follow it for over three-quarters of a mile to Cookham. On passing a boatyard, the path becomes macadamed and passes a riverside green. At the far end of this, turn right onto path C51 through a gate into the churchyard, passing the twelfth-century church with its fifteenth-century tower to the left and continuing out through another gate to the busy but narrow A4094. The village centre is to the right and is well worth a visit. Otherwise turn left and follow the A4094 over Cookham Bridge, built in 1867 to replace an earlier wooden structure, but now no longer suited to the amount of traffic it bears.

After passing a boatyard to the right, turn right through a derelict kissing-gate onto path WB1. Now bear half left across a field with a fine view of Tower Hill with its eighteenth-century folly, Hedsor Tower ahead to a stile near a bend in one of the four streams into which the Thames temporarily divides below Cookham Bridge. Cross this and take path HD1a, following the riverbank for a short distance. Where the river bears away to the right, leave it and go straight on across the field to a stile. Now follow a right-hand fence to a footbridge. Do not cross this, but instead turn sharp left onto path HD1, crossing the field to the corner of a hedge. Here keep straight on, following a right-hand hedge, swinging left then right around a small compound (now on path WB2) to reach a stile by a gate in the corner of the field leading to the A4094. Turn right onto the road, then immediately right again over a stile onto path WB3 into the next field. Bear half left across this, following a right-hand fence with views to your right of Hedsor Tower and the tiny hillside Hedsor Church further to your right to a kissing-gate into another road. Cross this and continue straight on along the concrete drive to Hollands Farm. At the farm go through a kissing-gate in the right-hand fence and bear slightly right along a raised track passing right of a cowshed then bearing slightly left to a kissing-gate in a corner of the field. Here follow a grassy bank beside a left-hand hedge, passing through further kissing-gates to reach the corner of an industrial estate. Now take path WB4, following the industrial estate fence and soon joining a concrete path alongside it. On reaching a stile, cross it, join a road and follow it straight on over a bridge over the River Wye to the A4094. Turn left onto this road and where it forks, take the A4155 straight on. Just before Lloyds Bank and a mini-roundabout, turn right onto bridleway WB25 back to your point of departure.

WALK 29:   Burnham Beeches

Length of Walk: 7.4 miles / 11.9 Km

Starting Point: Green gates near kiosk on Lord Mayor's Drive, Burnham Beeches.

Grid Ref: SU954850

Maps: OS Landranger Sheet 175
OS Explorer Sheet 3 (or old Pathfinder Sheet 1157 (SU88/98))
(small part only) Chiltern Society FP Map No.13

How to get there/Parking: The main parking area of Burnham Beeches, 3.1 miles south of Beaconsfield, may be reached from the town or Junction 2 of the M40 by taking the A355 southwards for over 3 miles to reach Farnham Common. Just before the start of the shopping parade, turn right onto a road signposted to Burnham Beeches. At a crossroads at the edge of the Beeches, go straight on along Lord Mayor's Drive and park about 300 yards along it.

Notes: Paths in this area tend to be boggy even in dry weather.

Burnham Beeches, which serve as a 'green lung' and wooded playground for London, its western suburbs and the nearby dormitory towns and villages, represent a milestone in British conservation history. Their purchase in 1878 by the Corporation of the City of London, together with the purchase of Epping Forest, shows public authority in Victorian England becoming aware of the need to conserve the countryside and take active steps to fulfil this requirement. Burnham Beeches also have a unique characteristic which is of interest to the countryman as well as the urban dweller: the gnarled ancient beeches which, in some cases, may be up to a thousand years old. They have survived this long because, until about 1820, they were regularly pollarded for firewood and for making charcoal. It is this treatment which has caused their fantastic shapes. The end result is that the Beeches resemble a primaeval forest and contrast sharply with modern managed woodlands.

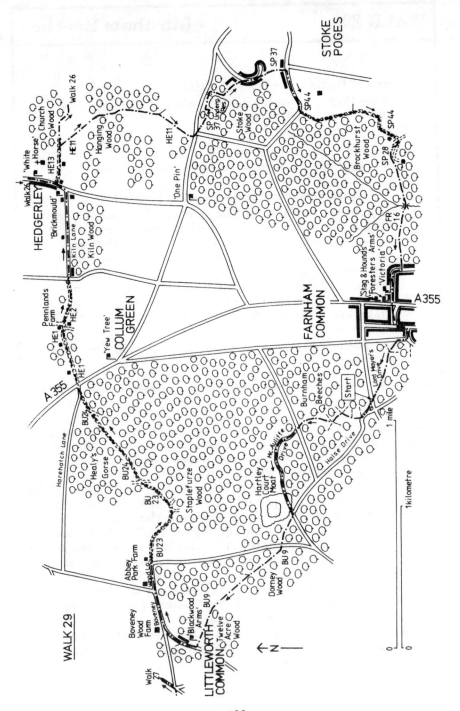

WALK 29

STOKE POGES

HEDGERLEY

COLLUM GREEN

FARNHAM COMMON

LITTLEWORTH COMMON

A355

←N

0 ____ 1 mile
0 ____ 1 kilometre

136

This walk is one of a particularly wooded nature, traversing the Beeches to Littleworth Common before passing through more woodland to cross the A355 near Collum Green. The next section visiting the picturesque rural village of Hedgerley is more open, before you return through more woods to Farnham Common and Burnham Beeches.

Starting from the green gates near the kiosk at the western end of the Lord Mayor's Drive parking area, continue straight on along the Drive for a few yards, then take the first forking road to the right, soon joining another road. At a left-hand bend, where Halse Drive is signposted, leave the road and take a path straight on into the woods, soon bearing right, ignoring a branching track to your right and starting to descend. Just before the path drops steeply to reach a stream, turn left onto a crossing path and follow it downhill and up again until you reach a five-way path junction. Here turn right onto a wide, gently climbing path and follow it straight on for some 300 yards to a road junction. Take Mc.Auliffe Drive straight on and follow it for nearly half a mile, looking out for an ancient earthwork known as Hartley Court Moat to your right, part of the outer mound of which crosses the road. This earthwork is believed to be the site of a mediaeval fortified homestead and farm. Just past this earthwork, at a road junction, turn right over a slight mound onto a macadam path flanked by rhododendrons. On reaching another road, cross it and take path BU9 straight on over a stile into Dorney Wood. Follow an obvious path straight on through the wood for quarter of a mile, ignoring branching paths to right and left and eventually leaving the wood through a kissing-gate. Now take a fenced path straight on between fields to cross a stile by a corner of Twelve Acre Wood and follow the edge of the wood to two gates and stiles leading to a road by the 'Blackwood Arms' at Littleworth Common.

Turn right onto this road and at a T-junction by Boveney Wood Farm, turn right into Boveney Wood Lane. At a further road junction, follow this lane straight on, then, at a sharp right-hand bend, leave it and take path BU23, a wide green lane, straight on. On reaching a stile and gates, cross the stile and follow a left-hand hedge to a stile and gates into Staplefurze Wood. In the wood, follow its inside edge for nearly quarter of a mile, ignoring branching paths to the right. When the path eventually leaves the edge of the wood, ignore a crossing track and take path BU24 straight on through the woods for nearly half a mile to reach a stile and gates. Cross the stile and continue straight on to reach a gate and stile into Harehatch Lane. Turn right onto this road and follow it to the A355 near Collum Green, then cross this busy road carefully and take bridleway HE1, a macadam private road, straight on to Pennlands Farm, once centre of the local brickmaking industry. Here take bridleway HE2, a fenced track, straight on, later becoming a hedged lane and reaching a road junction. Now take a path on the left-hand verge of Kiln Lane straight on, later rejoining the road and following it to the 'Brickmould' at Hedgerley with two wistarias on its walls and a weeping willow in front.

Turn left here into Village Lane, then, by the village noticeboard, turn right onto path HE13, a gravelly lane between the manor house and the attractive village pond (where you join Walk 26). Follow this lane straight on with views through the trees to your left of Hedgerley Church (see Walk 26) to reach a gate and stile at the far end of the lane. Cross the stile and (leaving Walk 26 again), bear half right onto path HE11 across a field to a stile into Hanging Wood just right of the far corner of the field. Now follow an obvious path straight on through the wood until you reach a stile. Cross this and turn right soon leaving the wood. Here follow a fenced path between fields straight on to reach another wood, then turn left over a footbridge into a corner of the wood, soon leaving it again by a stile. Now go straight on across the field to a gate and stile near a tall Scots pine on the edge of a wood ahead. Cross the stile and turn left onto a road. At a road junction, bear half right onto path SP37, the left-hand of two paths into Stoke Wood. Follow this straight on. On reaching a four-way path junction, bear left onto a path which eventually reaches the entrance to an underground reservoir. Cross this entrance, then turn right onto a fenced path, skirting the reservoir and then passing between gardens to reach a private road. Turn right onto this road and follow it for about 100 yards. Just past a house called 'Footprints', turn right into a narrow path between garden hedges (still SP37) and follow it to another road on the outskirts of Stoke Poges.

Turn right along this road and after some 300 yards, at a right-hand bend, turn left between bollards onto wide bridleway SP44, following the edge of Brockhurst Wood with views to your left towards Stoke Poges. After nearly half a mile, follow the bridleway turning right then left but still on the edge of the wood. On reaching a junction of tracks, bear half right onto path SP28, the drive to Hornbeam Cottage. By brick gateposts, cross a stile and follow a waymarked path parallel to the drive, then, where the drive turns left into a garden, take an obvious path straight on through beechwoods. After some 350 yards, cross a culvert and take path FR16 straight on between fences through the woods, later between gardens to reach Parsonage Lane at Farnham Common. Turn right onto this road, then, at a bend, turn left into Victoria Road to reach the A355. Cross this road and take a macadam path straight on, soon joining Kingsway. At road junctions, turn left into Green Lane, then right into Hawthorn Lane. At the edge of Burnham Beeches, turn right again into Bedford Drive and after about 90 yards, turn left onto a well-defined path through the trees which soon emerges into open grassland. Here bear half left, following a worn path along the edge of the grassland area to reach Lord Mayor's Drive near your point of departure.

WALK 30:   Stoke Poges

Length of Walk: 9.9 miles / 16.0 Km
Starting Point: Junction of B416 (Gerrards Cross Road) &
Pennylets Green, Stoke Poges.
Grid Ref: SU982844
Maps: OS Landranger Sheet 176
OS Pathfinder Sheet 1158 (TQ08/18) &
Explorer Sheet 3 (or old Pathfinder Sheet
1157 (SU88/98))
How to get there/Parking: Stoke Poges, 3 miles southwest
of Gerrards Cross, may be reached from the junction of the
A40 and B416 at Gerrards Cross Common, by taking the
B416 towards Slough for 2.8 miles. On reaching the
village, turn right into Pennylets Green for the Bell Hill
Shopping Centre car park.
Notes: Several parts of the walk tend to be swampy even in
dry weather.

Stoke Poges, the name of which derives from the
thirteenth-century marriage of the heiress of the manor,
Amice de Stoke, to her guardian's son, Sir Robert Pugeys, has
gone into history as the setting for Thomas Gray's 'Elegy
written in a Country Churchyard'. However the churchyard,
where it is believed to have been written, lies in fields
preserved by the National Trust more than a mile from the
modern village centre which bears little resemblance to the
rural idyll which Gray depicts.

The walk soon leaves this enclave of suburbia behind and
crosses the wooded Stoke Common, which was preserved for
the village in 1810 after a lengthy battle to prevent its
enclosure. You then pass through the picturesque village of
Fulmer and turn southwards to explore Black Park with its
attractive lake and fine coniferous woods and Langley Park
with some rare trees and its Georgian mansion, before
returning across country to Stoke Poges.

Starting from the junction of the B416 (Gerrards Cross Road) and Pennylets Green, take the B416 northwards for over quarter of a mile. Just past its junction with Vine Road, turn right through a gap by gates onto bridleway SP35, taking the right-hand track which follows a right-hand boundary mound marking the edge of Stoke Common. Follow this mound for three-quarters of a mile, turning sharp left after quarter of a mile. In places, it may be necessary to leave the mound for a few yards to circumvent swampy areas, but it should be kept in view to prevent your getting lost. Where the mound turns right by a hollybush, fork left away from it, ignoring a crossing path and taking a path straight on across the common, disregarding all branching and crossing tracks. Eventually you emerge at a road opposite Small Acres Pig Farm. Turn right onto this road and left at a road junction to reach the village of Fulmer, the name of which is a contraction of the mediaeval 'Fouwelemere' meaning 'lake of birds'. Despite its proximity to London, Fulmer, unlike most of its neighbours, has been allowed to survive largely unaltered with its attractive seventeenth-century church, eighteenth-century pub and two interesting manor houses nearby. The church, unusual for the Chilterns in being built of brick, was built by Sir Marmaduke Dayrell in 1610 and contains a monument to him.

Pass the pub and the church, then, by a telephone box, go through a kissing-gate by the gates to Muschamp Stud onto path FU2. Now take the stud drive straight on and where it turns right, leave it and take a fenced path straight on beside the concealed Alder Bourne, eventually passing through a copse to a gate and stile. Cross the stile and bear slightly left across a field to a gate and stile right of a telegraph pole. Having crossed the stile, bear slightly right to a kissing-gate just right of a corner of the field. Go through this, then bear slightly right, walking parallel to a hedge to your right, to a footbridge and kissing-gate into a clump of rhododendrons. Now go straight on through a 'tunnel' of rhododendrons, eventually joining a macadam drive at the edge of Home Wood. At a T-junction, take a path straight on through rhododendrons to reach another drive. Turn right onto this and where it forks, bear left and follow it straight on for 300 yards to reach a road.

Turn left onto this road and follow it straight on for over quarter of a mile, ignoring the branching Black Park Road and Cherry Tree Lane. About 100 yards past Cherry Tree Lane, opposite a house called Amberwood, turn right over a log into an entrance to the publicly-owned Black Park and take fenced bridleway WX23. At a three-way fork, turn right, soon veering left and following a right-hand ditch. Ignore a branching track to the left and at a T-junction, turn right, disregarding two branching paths to the left,

141

then, at a crossways, turn left leaving the bridleway and follow a wide stony track known as Queen's Drive for half a mile. At a clearing at the far end of this drive, take a path straight on, bearing slightly right. After a short distance, turn left to reach the shore of Black Park Lake, then turn right and follow a path along its shore to the far end of the lake. Here follow path WX4 round the end of the lake and continue past the refreshment kiosk and information centre. Where a wooden fence bars your way ahead, turn right, keeping right at a fork and following the fence of the information centre. By its back gates bear half left and take a track straight on through the woods for half a mile, disregarding all crossing tracks, until you reach the A412 dual-carriageway virtually opposite Billet Lane.

Cross this busy road carefully and follow Billet Lane straight on for quarter of a mile. Just before the first right-hand bend, just past the entrance to Highfield House on the left, turn right through a fence gap to enter Langley Park. Inside the park, bear left across an open grass area to the right-hand corner of a car park. Now take a path behind the car park parallel to Billet Lane and follow it for a third of a mile along an avenue of wellingtonias until you reach a gate and squeeze stile leading to a track. Cross the track and pass through a squeeze stile opposite, then follow an obvious path, gradually bearing left to a stile. Having crossed this, follow the wide fenced path WX10 between an orchard and open parkland. At the far end of this section, cross a stile and continue straight on. By the gates to Park Cottage, pass right of a garden wall and go straight on, following the wall to a further stile. Turn right over this onto fenced path WX12 and follow it, soon passing through a kissing-gate. Now continue straight on and soon Langley Park House can be seen some distance away to the right. This was built by the second Duke of Marlborough in the eighteenth century as a residence closer to London than Blenheim Palace. At the far side of the park, go through another kissing-gate into a lane and follow it straight on to a road junction at George Green, which was formerly known as Westmoor Green.

Here go straight on, wiggling slightly right into George Green Road. Follow this road through the village to the A412, then turn left along this road to reach a pedestrian flyover near the 'George'. Cross the flyover and retrace your steps on the other side of the road to a stile just before the 'Double Century'. Turn left over this and a second stile onto path WX7 and follow it straight on across a field to another stile. Cross this and go straight on to reach the fence of some gravel workings, then turn left and follow a gravel track to the far end of a long narrow field. Here turn right onto a wide fenced grassy track and follow it straight on for quarter of a mile. Where the track turns left and then right, follow it, then, where it forks, turn right over a

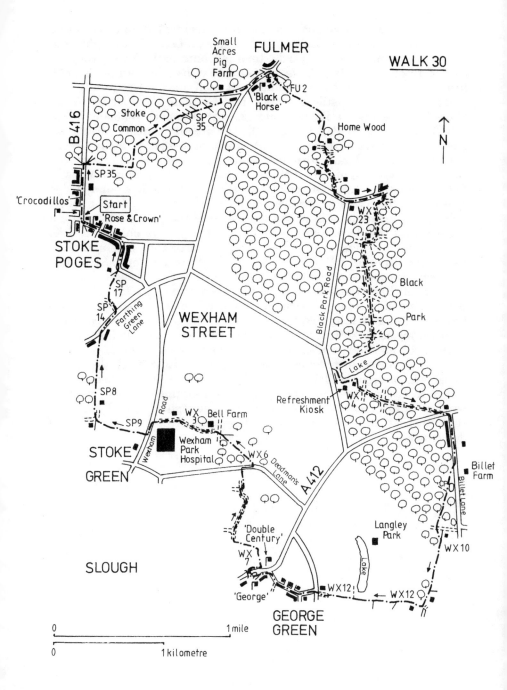

WALK 30

FULMER

Small Acres Pig Farm

'Black Horse'
FU 2

Home Wood

B 416

Stoke Common
SP 35

SP 35

'Crocodillos'

Start
'Rose & Crown'

STOKE POGES

SP 17

SP 14

Farthing Green Lane

WEXHAM STREET

WX 23

Black Park

Black Park Road

Lake

SP 8

SP 9

Wexham Road

WX 3

Bell Farm

Wexham Park Hospital

WX 6

Dedman's Lane

Refreshment Kiosk

WX 4

A 412

Billet Farm

Billet Lane

STOKE GREEN

Langley Park

WX 10

'Double Century'

WX 7

Lake

SLOUGH

'George'

WX 12

WX 12

GEORGE GREEN

0   1 mile

0   1 kilometre

footbridge onto a fenced path, immediately turning left and continuing for 250 yards to a stile leading to Deadman's Lane. Turn right onto this road, then, after 120 yards, turn left onto path WX6 through a belt of trees to a stile. Cross this and bear half left across a field, heading for distant farm buildings at Bell Farm. Eventually you emerge by way of a stile and gate into Gallions Lane by the farm. Cross the lane and a stile by a gate opposite onto path WX3 and follow this farm road past Bell Farm with its sixteenth-century farmhouse and Wexham Park Hospital to reach Wexham Road near Stoke Green.

Cross this road and turn left along its pavement for about 100 yards, then turn right over a stile onto path SP9. Go straight across a field to a stile under an oak tree, then follow a left-hand hedge straight on to cross a footbridge and stile. Here bear half right across a field to a gate and stile in the top corner of the field leading onto a drive. Cross the drive and a stile by a gate opposite onto path SP8. Now follow it beside a right-hand hedge to a further gate and stile. Cross the stile and follow a left-hand hedge straight on past a shed and then through two fields to a kissing-gate. Go through this and follow a left-hand fence straight on to cross a stile at the far side of the field, then follow a fenced path onto a macadam drive. Take this drive straight on to Farthing Green Lane, then turn right onto this road and follow it for some 200 yards. Now turn left over a stile by a gate onto path SP14 and follow a stony track ahead into a green lane. After about 130 yards, just before reaching a gate, turn right through a hedge gap onto path SP17 and head just left of the Victorian village school at Stoke Poges to reach a gate and kissing-gate leading to a bend in School Lane. Now follow this road straight on to a T-junction, then turn left into a road past the 'Rose and Crown' to your point of departure.

Books Published by
THE BOOK CASTLE

JOURNEYS INTO BEDFORDSHIRE: Anthony Mackay.
Foreword by The Marquess of Tavistock, Woburn Abbey.
A lavish book of over 150 evocative ink drawings.

A PILGRIMAGE IN HERTFORDSHIRE: H. M. Alderman.
Classic, between-the-wars tour round the county, embellished
with line drawings.

**COUNTRYSIDE CYCLING IN BEDFORDSHIRE,
BUCKINGHAMSHIRE and HERTFORDSHIRE:** Mick Payne.
Twenty rides on- and off-road for all the family.

LOCAL WALKS: South Bedfordshire and North Chilterns:
Vaughan Basham. Twenty-seven thematic circular walks.

LOCAL WALKS: North and Mid-Bedfordshire:
Vaughan Basham. Twenty-five thematic circular walks.

FAMILY WALKS: Chilterns South: Nick Moon.
Thirty 3 to 5 mile circular walks.

**CHILTERN WALKS: Hertfordshire, Bedfordshire and
North Buckinghamshire:** Nick Moon.
CHILTERN WALKS: Buckinghamshire: Nick Moon.
**CHILTERN WALKS: Oxfordshire and
West Buckinghamshire:** Nick Moon.
A trilogy of circular walks, in association with the Chiltern
Society. Each volume contains thirty circular walks.

**OXFORDSHIRE WALKS:
Oxford, the Cotswolds and the Cherwell Valley:** Nick Moon.
**OXFORDSHIRE WALKS:
Oxford, the Downs and the Thames Valley:** Nick Moon.
Two volumes that complement Chiltern Walks: Oxfordshire
and complete coverage of the county, in association with the
Oxford Fieldpaths Society. Thirty circular walks in each.

**FOLK: Characters and Events in the History
of Bedfordshire and Northamptonshire:** Vivienne Evans.
Anthology about people of yesteryear – arranged alphabetically
by village or town.

**LEGACIES:
Tales and Legends of Bedfordshire and Hertfordshire:**
Vic Lea. Twenty-five mysteries and stories based on fact,
including Luton Town Football Club. Many photographs.

MANORS and MAYHEM, PAUPERS and POLITICS:
Tales from Four Shires: Beds., Bucks., Herts.,
and Northants.: John Houghton.
Little-known historical snippets and stories.

MYTHS and WITCHES, PEOPLE and POLITICS:
Tales from Four Shires: Bucks., Beds., Herts.,
and Northants.: John Houghton.
Anthology of strange but true historical events.

ECCENTRICS and VILLAINS, HAUNTINGS and HEROES:
Tales from Four Shires: Northants., Beds.,
Bucks., and Herts.: John Houghton.
True incidents and curious events covering one thousand years.

THE RAILWAY AGE IN BEDFORDSHIRE: Fred Cockman.
Classic, illustrated acount of early railway history.

CHILTERN ARCHAEOLOGY: RECENT WORK:
A Handbook for the Next Decade: edited by Robin Holgate.
The latest views, results and excavations by twenty-three
leading archaeologists throughout the Chilterns.

WHIPSNADE WILD ANIMAL PARK: 'MY AFRICA': Lucy Pendar.
Foreword by Andrew Forbes. Introduction by Gerald Durrell.
Inside story of sixty years of the Park's animals and people –
full of anecdotes, photographs and drawings.

DUNSTABLE WITH THE PRIORY, 1100–1550: Vivienne Evans.
Dramatic growth of Henry I's important new town around a
major crossroads.

DUNSTABLE DECADE: THE EIGHTIES:
A Collection of Photographs: Pat Lovering.
A souvenir book of nearly 300 pictures of people and events in
the 1980s.

DUNSTABLE IN DETAIL: Nigel Benson.
A hundred of the town's buildings and features, plus town trail
map.

OLD DUNSTABLE: Bill Twaddle.
A new edition of this collection of early photographs.

BOURNE and BRED:
A Dunstable Boyhood Between the Wars: Colin Bourne.
An elegantly written, well-illustrated book capturing the spirit
of the town over fifty years ago.

ROYAL HOUGHTON: Pat Lovering.
Illustrated history of Houghton Regis from the earliest times to
the present.

BEDFORDSHIRE'S YESTERYEARS Vol. 1:
The Family, Childhood and Schooldays:
Brenda Fraser-Newstead.
Unusual early 20th century reminiscences, with private photographs.

BEDFORDSHIRE'S YESTERYEARS Vol. 2:
The Rural Scene: Brenda Fraser-Newstead.
Vivid first-hand accounts of country life two or three generations ago.

BEDFORDSHIRE'S YESTERYEARS Vol. 3:
Craftsmen and Trades People:
Brenda Fraser-Newstead.
Fascinating recollections over several generations practising many vanishing crafts and trades.

BEDFORDSHIRE'S YESTERYEARS Vol. 4:
War Times and Civil Matters:
Brenda Fraser-Newstead.
Two World Wars, plus transport, law and order, etc.

THE CHANGING FACE OF LUTON:
An Illustrated History:
Stephen Bunker, Robin Holgate and Marian Nichols.
Luton's development from earliest times to the present busy industrial town. Illustrated in colour and monochrome. The three authors from Luton Museum are all experts in local history, archaeology, crafts and social history.

THE MEN WHO WORE STRAW HELMETS:
Policing Luton, 1840–1974: Tom Madigan.
Meticulously chronicled history; dozens of rare photographs; author served in Luton Police for nearly fifty years.

BETWEEN THE HILLS:
The Story of Lilley, a Chiltern Village: Roy Pinnock.
A priceless piece of our heritage – the rural beauty remains but the customs and way of life described here have largely disappeared.

GLEANINGS REVISITED:
Nostalgic Thoughts of a Bedfordshire's Farmer's Boy:
E W O'Dell.
His own sketches and early photographs adorn this lively account of rural Bedfordshire in days gone by.

FARM OF MY CHILDHOOD, 1925–1947: Mary Roberts.
An almost vanished lifestyle on a remote farm near Flitwick.

THE VALE OF THE NIGHTINGALE:
The True Story of a Harpenden Family: Molly Andrews.
Victorian times to the present day in this lovely village.

THE TALL HITCHIN SERGEANT:
A Victorian Crime Novel based on fact: Edgar Newman.
Mixes real police officers and authentic background with an
exciting storyline.

THE TALL HITCHIN INSPECTOR'S CASEBOOK:
A Victorian Crime Novel based on fact: Edgar Newman.
Worthies of the time encounter more archetypal villains.

LEAFING THROUGH LITERATURE: Writer's Lives
in Hertfordshire and Bedfordshire: David Carroll.
Illustrated short biographies of many famous authors and their
connections with these counties.

THE HILL OF THE MARTYR: An Architectural History
of St. Albans Abbey: Eileen Roberts.
Scholarly and readable chronological narrative history of
Hertfordshire and Bedfordshire's famous cathedral. Fully
illustrated with photographs and plans.

SPECIALLY FOR CHILDREN

VILLA BELOW THE KNOLLS:
A Story of Roman Britain: Michael Dundrow.
An exciting adventure for young John in Totternhoe and
Dunstable two thousand years ago.

ADVENTURE ON THE KNOLLS:
A Story of Iron Age Britain: Michael Dundrow.
Excitement on Totternhoe Knolls as ten-year-old John finds
himself back in those dangerous times, confronting Julius
Caesar and his army.

THE RAVENS:
One Boy Against the Might of Rome: James Dyer.
On the Barton Hills and in the south-east of England as the
men of the great fort of Ravensburgh (near Hexton) confront
the invaders.

Further titles are in preparation.
All the above are available via any bookshop, or from the
publisher and bookseller

THE BOOK CASTLE
12 Church Street, Dunstable Bedfordshire, LU5 4RU
Tel: (01582) 605670